BIG BUCKS
THE BENOIT WAY

SECRETS FROM AMERICA'S FIRST FAMILY
OF WHITETAIL HUNTING

BRYCE TOWSLEY

Published by

krause
publications

700 E. State Street • Iola, WI 54990-0001
Telephone: 715/445-2214

Please call or write for our free catalog.
Our toll-free number to place an order or obtain a free catalog is 800-258-0929
or please use our regular business telephone 715-445-2214
for editorial comment and further information.

Library of Congress Catalog Number: 98-84440
ISBN: 0-87341-655-4

Printed in the United States of America

Some product names in this book are the registered trademarks of their respective companies.

Gore-Tex®	Cordora®	Beef-a-Roni®
Nike®	Duofold®	Bic®
Coke®	Sorel®	Zippo®
Thinsulate™	Core-Lokt®	Garmin®

Dedication

For my wife Robin.
Without you I wouldn't be a writer.
Actually, without you I wouldn't be much of anything.

From the Benoit family:
For Dick Duffy, a good friend whose final season came too soon.

From Lanny, Lane, and Shane:
To our mother, Iris Benoit, for all of her support and dedication through the years.

Foreword

It's ironic that one of the men most responsible for spurring deer hunting's popularity and its vast influence on the hunting industry maintains a low profile despite high name and face recognition.

Then again, that's probably Larry Benoit's intention. I've never met Benoit, but I sense he knows he's an excellent deer hunter and doesn't need to prove his skills to anyone. He's also tasted the celebrity lifestyle enough to realize he has more important matters to address. Besides, without trying, he attracts as much public attention as he can probably stomach.

Chances are, if you've been hunting deer a few years, you've somehow heard of Larry Benoit and his deer hunting family. Maybe you can even picture them as they first appeared in *Sports Afield* magazine in 1970: A family of hunters in green plaid with Remington pump-actions, and a line of big bucks hanging behind them on their home's porch.

Back then, my Wisconsin friends and I often talked about the Benoits and their hunting tactics as we sat around the kitchen table at night. I wish now I had kept my copy of those old *Sports Afield* magazines. I don't think I'm exaggerating when I say the Benoit articles were a landmark in deer huntings surge to prominence in North America. Just about the time I realized those magazines might be worth preserving on a bookshelf, they disappeared in the family's recycling bin. Yes, some of us lived in cities with recycling programs in the early 1970s!

A few years later I saw an advertisement for a book club, and noticed Benoit's face and name on one of the selections. He had helped write a book: *How to Bag the Biggest Buck of Your Life.* I joined the club instantly to get the book.

I don't recall the names of the other three books that came with the offer, but I guess it doesn't matter. I wanted Benoit's book, and I knew I would never loan it to anyone, even family members who didn't share the same roof. Only once has his book been out of my possession, and that was to ship it to Larry in 1996 for his autograph. Even now I can picture the spot where it sits on my bookshelves, just as I can remember where I stored it in my bunk/locker while I was in the Navy.

Shortly after going to work for *Deer & Deer Hunting* magazine in January 1991, I again realized I wasn't the only deer hunter who recalled the Benoit name from the 1970s. While looking for a quote to accompany a now-forgotten photo for a magazine article, I pulled out my copy of Benoit's book, found a passage I liked, and reprinted it atop the photo.

Soon after that magazine went out to our readers, we began hearing from people who wanted to know where they could buy Benoit's book. They remembered the Benoits from those old *Sports Afield* articles, but somehow they didn't know he had collaborated on a book in 1975. When informed that the book was long out of print and that even Benoit didn't have any to sell, several readers asked, Whatever became of him? I only knew Benoit and his family were still tracking and shooting bucks in the big woods of Maine and Vermont.

About four years ago, after getting to know Vermont outdoors writer Bryce Towsley, I asked if he knew the Benoits. Before long, Towsley had an assignment from me for *Deer & Deer Hunting:* Answer our readers question: Where are you now, Larry Benoit?

Bryce answered that question thoroughly in the January 1997 issue of *Deer & Deer Hunting,* but we knew before the article was published that it wouldn't satisfy Benoit's many fans. We continued to field calls inquiring where they could track down a copy of *How to Bag the Biggest Buck of Your Life.* No matter how often we told people the book was unavailable, they continued to hope Benoit had hidden a cache of books in his garage, basement, or some trunk buried under an old spruce.

Because there simply is no such stash, Krause Publications commissioned Towsley to write the book you now hold. We hope *Big Bucks the Benoit Way* will be just as instructive and entertaining as *How to Bag the Biggest Buck of Your Life.* With this book, though, you'll benefit from nearly 25 more years of the Benoit family's hunting experience. Each of the Benoits, whether it's Larry or his sons Lanny, Shane, and Lane, has slightly different skills and methods that they tailor-fit to make themselves better deer hunters. Perhaps you'll see some of your own traits in one of the Benoits, and try to blend their approach with your own.

But if you still can't match the Benoits' success, don't blame them. Appreciate them. They've earned their deer. And they've earned their accolades, even if they haven't sought them. Enjoy the book.

Patrick Durkin
Editor, *Deer & Deer Hunting*

Contents

Introduction

The magazine cover caused quite a stir when it hit the stands back in 1970. Deer hunters in general take a lot of pride in their skills and tend to be a bit competitive, so when the cover of a *Sports Afield* magazine asked the question, "Larry Benoit—is he the best deer hunter in America?," most hunters took notice and a few took offense. The hunters I was running with at the time soon discovered that Larry was from our home state of Vermont and our skepticism quickly turned to pride. He was one of us and we soon enough decided he was indeed the best.

The many magazine articles, speaking engagements, and the 1975 book that followed answered the question for the rest of the world and established Larry Benoit as the "real deal." Anyone who hunted deer understood that Larry knew his stuff and he soon became well known throughout the whitetail hunting scene as a premiere hunter and teacher about whitetail deer.

His influence regionally was incredible as it seemed that every hunter in the north woods was dressed in green plaid wool and was carrying a Remington pump-action rifle. Larry's first book *How to Bag the Biggest Buck of Your Life* sold at an astonishing rate and even today, with it many years out of print, he receives inquiries almost daily. Those who have copies guard them well and anybody lucky enough to find one on a used book shelf grabs it, regardless of the price. It ranks in the minds of many as one of the classics of whitetail deer hunting books and as a "must have" in any whitetail library.

We hunters were eager for hard-core deer hunting information and we wanted the long-promised second hunting book, but it didn't materialize. There was a taste of it with Larry's autobiography published in 1992, but while it contained deer hunting stories, it wasn't a deer hunting book. For a variety of reasons, two and a half decades slipped past. A lot changed in that time.

The whitetail deer ascended to the throne of the number one big game animal in North America and perhaps the world, nothing else even comes close. As a result, the business of whitetail deer hunting has flourished at an unprecedented rate. More hunting celebrities burst onto the scene, some very real and some pretenders. Several magazines devoted to deer hunting started publishing, many are gone, but some have remained and prospered. Hunting videos and television shows have brought deer hunting into America's living room and entire industries have sprung up to feed the deer hunter's insatiable appetite for more and more tools and information for and about hunting whitetail deer. Tree stands, camouflage, scents, and calls all have flourished during that time. The archery industry grew and expanded, as did the muzzle loader industry, both driven primarily by the whitetail deer hunter. Gun manufacturers changed their product lines and marketing direction to reflect the impact that the whitetail deer hunter was having on their businesses. The ammo companies developed more and better bullets and cartridges, many designed specifically for hunting deer. And the whitetail deer hunters themselves discovered the grand world beyond the back forty as more and more of us traveled to distant lands in search of bigger bucks and larger adventures.

All the while the Benoits continued doing what they have always done. Each fall they fill their tags with the biggest and the best bucks from what may well be one of the most difficult regions of the country in which to hunt deer. They continued to astonish their critics and the whitetail world with their expertise and their incredible success at bending the game pole to the point of breaking. As their skills in the big woods grew even more legendary, they teased us with a seminar or magazine article here and there, but still no book emerged. There were a few false starts, several times hopes were raised, only to be dashed and the secrets for the most part remained theirs alone.

Then one night my phone rang. It was Shane Benoit asking if I would be interested in meeting with him to talk about writing the book. I was honored, humbled, and terrified. At first I almost said no, that I was too busy. I, like the rest of my peers, wanted this book badly, but the thought that I might be asked to write it left me questioning if I was up to the task.

I had been writing for several years—the last few full time—and publishing in a variety of outdoor

1972 Vermont bucks. Photo courtesy The Vermont Sportsman.

magazines. While I have nightmares about being reduced to writing on one topic, it would seem boring and mundane enough to drive me back to a real job, I suppose that I had emerged in the minds of many readers as a "whitetail" writer. I had plans for a couple of books, but this one was different, this was the "Benoit Book" that we had all been talking about for years.

Obviously, in the end I agreed. I felt strongly that it was a book that needed to be written and that somebody had to write it. I remembered well Ronald Reagan asking, "If not now—when? If not us—who?" It was a concept that I believed in and because I did, I knew the answer. I came to see it as a challenge and I also saw it as an opportunity to learn and to study with the masters.

The man likely most responsible for this book becoming a reality is Pat Durkin, the editor of *Deer & Deer Hunting* Magazine. He and I were bunking together in 1994 while on a Mississippi deer hunt. We were lying awake one night talking quietly, as hunters in camps around the world often do, when Pat suggested I write an article on the Benoits for the magazine. It ran in the January 1997 issue and I suppose everyone involved was satisfied, because it was shortly after that when Shane called. Pat then hooked me up with the Krause book division and put in a word or two about the viability of the project, which I am sure fueled its launch.

What resulted was this book.

That statement seems a bit meager, though. This was an undertaking of proportions such as I had never involved myself in, and at times it was overwhelming. There were some major problems that kept me from the computer for weeks and months all the while the deadline loomed, but I'll not bore you with those details. What really resulted was so much more than just a book. I developed a respect and friendship for the Benoit family, particularly Shane and Larry who worked closest with me to make this a success. After three decades of hunting whitetails all across North America I thought I knew a thing or two about deer and the sport of deer hunting, but the Benoits showed me how little I really did know. It was, I am sure, never their intent to do so, but it's like my Uncle Butch used to say when talking about the Benoits, "Every sport has it superstars." Like superstars everywhere, they make the difficult look easy and they unknowingly and unwillingly make the rest of us all too aware of our inadequacies.

What is great, though, about the Benoit family is that not only are they superstars of whitetail hunting, but they are all too willing to share with you how they do it, which is the reason for this book's existence. It's not likely that we can all become as good as they are, but then we all can't learn to play basketball like Michael Jordan either. What we can do is to listen and learn, apply what we learned to become the best hunters that we can be and then hopefully one day pass that knowledge on to another young deer hunter.

What I would ask is that you not only learn from this book, but that you take some pleasure in reading it as well. And that you do the same with your approach to whitetail deer hunting. That you make the goal not only to bag the biggest buck of your life, but to learn to enjoy the chase that will someday lead you to that goal. Truly the real essence of hunting trophy whitetail bucks is not in killing the deer, but hunting him.

Chapter 1

The First Family of Deer Hunting

"As far as I am concerned there is nothing like a whitetail buck, a big dominant buck. A buck like that is majestic and proud. He is his own boss and he answers to no one."

-Larry Benoit

Larry (left) and Lanny Benoit in the early years. Benoit photo.

I have a rather modest collection of sporting magazines that starts back in the early years of this century and continues through the years of my youth, which arguably ended in the early seventies. (My wife and a few others contend that I never grew up, but that's not to debate here.) In comparing those classic publications with today's "hook and bullet" journals, the most glaring difference is in the almost total lack of whitetail hunting articles in those older publications.

We hunters and readers of the time always knew what the editors did not, that even back then the premier big game animal in America was the whitetail deer. It was hunted in more places and by more people than any other North American big game species. How could there not be a widespread interest lurking deep and waiting release? It was, of course, a gut feeling; we didn't have the benefit of the "demographic studies" that the magazines used, but there was never any doubt that the whitetail explosion was somewhere in our future.

So when the September 1970 issue of *Sports Afield* magazine carried an ominous and vaguely frightening cover photo of a man in a green plaid

Left to right: Shane, Larry, Lane, and Lanny in 1980. Benoit photo.

hat staring through a peep sight and down a rifle barrel directly into your eyes, it commanded attention. The line below the magazine title read "Larry Benoit—is he the best deer hunter in America?" Many who read that story and the books and articles that followed concluded that perhaps he was.

It might be argued that this magazine cover and article helped to launch one of the first whitetail hunting superstars and to release upon us the beginnings of the whitetail boom. Larry's star shone brightly for many years, but it likely reached its crescendo with the release of his book *How to Bag the Biggest Buck of Your Life* in 1975. Even today, with the last copy sold years ago and no reprint imminent, Larry continues to receive calls requesting the book. And why not? Who among us can look at that cover photo of Larry dressed in his trademark green plaid wool, holding his Remington 760 carbine in one hand and the massive antler of a huge, hog-nosed, bull-shouldered northern whitetail buck in the other and not want a copy of our own?

The influence of the Benoits on a generation of hunters is seen throughout the Northeastern woods in the many hunters dressed in green checkered wool and rubber boots with Remington pump-action rifles in their hands. I too can trace my love of these rifles to Larry. Long before I ever met the man, I bought my beloved .30-06, mostly because he used one. Like so much else from Larry, I found that he was right. He was right about the wool and right about the gun. They are simply the best choices for hunting in the thick, cold, and wet woods of the Northeast. As a benefit of being a gun writer, it would seem that these days I have some of the finest rifles on the market in my gun room, but when I am hunting the thick woods of home

Lanny's 9-point, 215-pound buck (left) and Larry's 13-point, 215-pound buck from 1972 (Maine). Benoit photo.

and it is getting time to finish the job, it is that worn old 760 that travels with me into the gray cold of a November dawn.

The way the Benoits hunt is often considered "regional," and to some extent it is. They are trackers. But even more important is that they are woodsmen. They have a profound understanding of the trophy whitetail buck. They know how he thinks and how he will act. While many think that they simply get on the track of a big buck and "run him down," nothing could be further from the truth. It takes an overall woodsman with a profound understanding of white-tail behavior, particularly big buck behavior, because they do indeed act differently than all of the other deer in the woods, to succeed at hunting deer this way. The fact that they take lots of their bucks on bare-ground will attest to that. Sure they are trackers, but more than that, they are deer hunters, the truest form of deer hunters. They will enter the whitetail's woods and hunt him on his terms. They disdain tree stands and watching trails. They don't rattle horns, make drives, or blow calls. The only scent they will admit to using is "common sense." Instead, they move through the woods on the deer's turf and in his domain. It is one on one, man against deer, arguably the purest form of deer hunting. Most agree it is also the most difficult.

I have been blessed with the opportunity to have hunted whitetails throughout much of North America. I have visited most of the well-known areas and I have tried just about every method invented to hunt whitetails. If there is a tougher style or place to hunt trophy bucks than how and where the Benoits

hunt, I have yet to encounter it. Yet they would have it no other way. They have opportunities to hunt in other places, but they like the freedom and challenge of the north woods and hunt there by choice. They still identify a trophy buck by the traditional northeastern measure of "200 pounds or more dressed weight" and it is a rare season when each and every one of the Benoits doesn't take a buck exceeding that standard.

Larry (left) and Lanny Benoit with some bucks shot in the mid-1970s. Benoit photo.

They hunt in the big country of northern Maine where deer densities are low and there are often miles and miles of empty country between trophy bucks. For many hunters this is perhaps the most frustrating and difficult place in the whitetail's domain to hunt for trophy bucks. While Maine's reputation for big-bodied bucks is well deserved, they are still as rare there as an honest politician. Success rates are in the single digits and it is not uncommon for many hunters to spend the entire month-long season without seeing a buck of any kind. Yet the Benoit family will find and take the best of the best from these vast woods with apparent ease. But, apparent only to the outside observer, those who have hunted here know the difficulty of taking big bucks, and those who know the Benoit family will recognize how much of themselves they put into this sport.

While these days it seems that everybody who ever shot a decent buck is now a bona fide expert and on the seminar trail, Larry has been pretty quiet. I am honored to now call him my friend and I have spent hours and hours talking with him and his family about what deer hunting has become and where they think it is going.

Larry still lives in the same north-central Vermont home where he and Iris, his wife of 56 years, raised nine children. It is not big and certainly not fancy, but it states the obvious—that Larry places his values in things less tangible than the materialistic pursuit that so many of us find ourselves caught up in each day. Having come of age in the great depression and grown to manhood in the CCC camps of that time, he knows about the value of things in life. It wasn't easy raising this large of a family on a working man's income; it took hard

A young Larry Benoit with some Vermont Bucks. Benoit photo.

Handmade knives for sale in Larry Benoit's living room along with a wall full of trophy whitetail antlers. Bryce M. Towsley photo.

Trophy whitetails line one wall in Larry Benoit's living room. Bryce M. Towsley photo.

work and long hours. That Yankee work ethic was instilled in his offspring and it has insured that each grew to adulthood and has prospered in their own way. But, the one thing that remained even more sacred than work to much of the family was deer hunting.

Stepping into this house will stagger most hunters—it's like a whitetail shrine. One wall of the living room is completely covered with big racks that are packed so tightly that it is hard to define a single set of antlers from the whole. It is nothing but a wall of tines that is easy to imagine stretching on to infinity. The opposing wall is filled with mounted heads of more Jurassic whitetails. Between are rifles along the beams in the ceiling, Native American art (reflecting Larry's pride in his Iroquois heritage), and a room that has obviously seen a lot of family, love, and life. Everywhere you look there are more hunting treasures, photos of the great

days and the great bucks, Larry's handmade knives, and antlers, always antlers. The house alone helps you to understand that the success of the Benoits starts with the fact that they as a family are defined by and aligned with the whitetail deer. Seeing this house and knowing this family is to understand that to separate the Benoits from deer hunting would sever their souls.

This was defined well to me as I sat at the kitchen table (every home I have ever felt welcome and comfortable in used the kitchen table as its social gathering place) with Shane and Larry. We were talking about tactics, and they were explaining about the final minutes of the hunt—the time when you know you are close to the buck and everything depends on the next few moves. It's the most dangerous point in any hunt, the time when the senses of both the hunter and the hunted are tuned to their finest, the time that determines who wins and who

Left to right: Larry, Uncle Windy, and Lanny. Benoit photo.

loses. It's also the time when things go wrong. It's when most hunters get antsy and blow it. But they have a way to deal with it.

They call it the "death creep," not so much for the expected demise of the buck, but because the hunter must move so slowly as to almost appear to be a corpse. It's when the hunter is moving in for the kill, when the buck has all of the aces and the hunter is most likely to make a mistake.

Shane and Larry both were describing to me the necessity of maintaining complete focus.

"Your thoughts must be only and totally on the task at hand," one of them said. "You must think of nothing else but seeing that buck before he knows you have."

They explained how you must draw yourself in and approach a "Zen" (my word) state of total concentration.

"How do you maintain this, particularly when it must continue sometimes for hours?" I asked.

"How can I not?" replied Larry. "There is nothing I love more in life."

Larry is 73 years old and he took his first whitetail at the age of 7, his first 200-pound buck at 9, and has taken countless more in the years that followed.

"Haven't you become jaded?" I asked. "Having done it all and for so many years, don't you find it hard to maintain the 'fire in your belly' that it takes for this kind of effort?"

Larry looked at me like I was the dumbest man on earth.

"I love whitetails and deer hunting. That hasn't faded and never will until I am laid in the ground to rest. Maintaining the drive, the focus, the love for deer hunting is as easy for me as breathing.

"As far as I am concerned there is nothing like a whitetail buck, a big dominant buck. A buck like that is majestic and proud. He is his own boss and he answers to no one.

"You don't get those big bucks every day. Many hunters will spend years and years and never shoot one. We don't hunt for competitiveness; if we can't take the buck we want we won't shoot one. We don't shoot the small bucks just to take a deer, we

let them grow and perhaps we will find them in a few years as bigger bucks.

"We also honor the buck. We have a tradition to keep the spirit of the deer with us. Part of that is in the blood that I put on my face after the kill, which is a tradition in our family, but also in the piece of a buck's ear that I keep on my gun. It serves as a talisman, but it's also to keep the spirit of the deer with me on the hunt. Because a deer hears better than any animal in the woods, my Indian ancestors tied a piece of a deer's ear to their bows for good luck. I have one on my rifle for the same reason.

"We also do not hang a buck by his neck. I think that's degrading to the buck, and he is too majestic an animal, even in death, to humiliate him in that way."

Larry with a buck his brother shot in 1953. Benoit photo.

A young Lanny Benoit with some Vermont bucks in 1969. Benoit photo.

When Larry talks about "we" he means the family, for it would be hard to separate the two. This is particularly apparent in deer hunting. Three of Larry's sons, Lanny, Shane, and Lane, are as tuned in their lives to deer hunting as is Larry. When they are not there to hear him say it, Larry will tell you with obvious pride that they are better hunters than he is. Part of that is fatherly pride, but most is simply the truth as he sees it. Many of those antlers on the walls are trophies taken by the sons.

Over the years each has developed his own hunting style. For example, even at 52, Lanny's long legs and wandering spirit make him a "ranger" who will travel miles and miles

Lanny Benoit "dragging one out." This 1997 buck weighed 210 pounds and had 9 points. Benoit photo.

each day in pursuit of his bucks. He will strike off into the woods with little concern for where it will all end. He will go for miles and miles, taking in stride whatever comes his way. He may be a county away from his truck at dark, but he will deal with that then. He will cover lots of territory in search of a good buck track and he will go into places that other hunters shun. He will take chances by traveling into places that others will not and they often pay off when he finds the tracks of a big buck.

This intense focus and drive has allowed him to rise to the top of skeet shooting and snowmobile racing, but it is truly deer hunting that drives him. I have hunted with Lanny a little, and while he appears on the surface to be laid back and calm, in reality he is focused and driven. Most of the family would agree that he is the best hunter. Larry said that he is the best deer hunter alive today, and I find little to argue with that statement. When he

hits a track nothing can deter him; he is like a hound dog on the trail, and that buck is in big trouble. Lanny is big, fast, aggressive, and very sure of himself. He carries that into his approach to deer hunting and makes it work for him. He hunts hard and fast, and many of his bucks are running when he shoots at them. But that is little problem to a man who shoots as well as he does.

He is modest about it, saying it's a lucky shot, but the truth is that he has a lot of "lucky shots" to his credit. In 1997 he spotted a big 9-point buck traveling though the hardwoods nearly 200 yards off. He found a lane that he called a "bowling alley," but was really much smaller, and he killed that buck when it came through it. It was a tough shot, one that most hunters wouldn't have attempted, much less made, but that night at camp he told me, "I just got lucky." Somehow I don't think that luck had much to do with it.

A couple of good Vermont bucks taken in 1980: 225 pounds (Larry's; left) and 230 pounds (Lanny's). Benoit photo.

Another time I dropped him and his son Landon off on a big track early one morning and drove the rig around to another road to hunt myself. It was less than 45 minutes after starting that track when I was just leaving the truck and heard them shooting. They were in brush so thick that seeing past a few feet would be hard and putting a bullet any farther all but impossible. The shots were fast and frequent. Fifteen minutes later there was another barrage and this time I heard the distinct sound of a bullet striking the deer. I didn't even bother loading my rifle, I just started the rig and went to pick them and the buck up.

Landon is Lanny's oldest son. At 23 years old he is proof that the need to deer hunt is inbred and able to cross generational lines. He is long-legged, tall, and slender. With the energy and conditioning of youth, combined with his long strides, he is a match for Lanny in the woods. They hunt to-gether and they cover a lot of territory. One day in 1997 the GPS said that they were 14 miles from the rig when they quit for the day. That's in a straight line, because GPS doesn't take into account terrain variations and certainly adds nothing for the meandering way a deer track covers ground. I would guess that you could easily add several more miles to the actual route that got them there. The only way back was to walk, and they did, all the way back to the rig. They both looked in pretty good shape when they got to the camp late that night. I suspect by then most us would have been in a coma.

Landon is quiet, preferring to spend his spare time reading rather than talking. But, that quiet nature hides the heart of a competitor. He is a force to reckon with on the snowmobile race tracks and in the whitetail woods with an admirable collection of big bucks to his credit already.

Landon Benoit with a 194-pound, 8-point buck (1995). Benoit photo.

Lane is 43 years old and his vanity license plate reads "Slammer," his nickname, which is an apt description of him—he is not a guy you want to get in the way of. He too is aggressive and hard driving when it comes to deer hunting, and I can easily believe that many of his deer are a result of his sheer force of determination and will. He works hard from dawn to dark and takes it all very seriously. He has emerged as the bare-ground expert and has managed to track and take some impressive bucks without snow. He currently holds the family record for the biggest deer with a field dressed weight of 284 pounds.

Shane is the youngest at 41. He is quiet, mild mannered, and in may ways very different than his brothers. He is as passive as they are aggressive, except when it comes to deer hunting. Shane is quietly accepting of his own skills, which are very impressive, but is very focused and driven during hunting season.

"Everybody likes Shane," Larry told me. "They always have."

Shane's hunting style is a little slower and more methodical; he still covers lots of ground, but he is thinking all the while. I have watched him puzzle out a track that would have had many hunters giving up in frustration. But, he stayed with it and had us back on the buck so fast that I didn't even realize what happened until later.

He and Larry are inseparable during the deer season and they often will "double team" their bucks, which is covered in some detail in Chapter 12.

Lane with an 8-point, 243-pound buck taken in 1986. Photo courtesy Glen Schwartz.

Shane Benoit with his first Maine buck over 200 pounds. The 8-point weighed 207 pounds and was taken on bare ground in 1978. Benoit photo.

Shane with a 224-pound, 10-point buck he shot in 1989. Benoit photo.

Larry Benoit on a buck's track in 1997. Bryce M. Towsley photo.

Some bucks from Maine, 1991. Benoit photo.

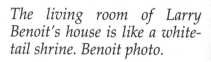

The living room of Larry Benoit's house is like a whitetail shrine. Benoit photo.

Larry is the kingpin of it all. The "boys" call him "Pop," and he still spends the entire month-long deer season in Maine, hunting hard every day. I asked him about hunting and tracking at 73 years of age.

Leo Benoit, Larry's father. Benoit photo.

"I can still track," he told me. "But I have slowed down some. I have learned that as my body ages I must hunt more with my head. I am more particular about what track I will take. Now I don't just look for a track that is so hot it's smoking, I look for a track with fire in it. That's a buck I can catch and kill."

Their records speak for themselves. They hunt only Maine these days and are allowed just one buck each annually. Between 1989 and 1995 the five of them (including Lanny's son Landon) have held a total of 35 Maine buck tags. They filled 28 of them with deer that have an aggregate total dressed weight of 6,132 pounds. That is an average dressed weight of more than 218 pounds, while the antlers averaged 8.5 points. (They have never scored any of their bucks for Boone & Crockett or any other record book.)

Larry's bucks in that time have had an average dressed weight of 215.1 pounds and the antlers have averaged 8.5 points. Lanny's bucks average weight is a whopping 239.3 pounds! The antlers on Lanny's deer have averaged 8.1 points. Shane's deer have a weight average of 221.6 and the antler's 8.6 points. Lane's bucks have an average dressed weight of 213.2 pounds and antlers averaging 8.5 points. Landon averaged 201.4 pounds and 8.4 points.

I doubt that many families can match this record of taking trophy bucks anywhere they are hunted and particularly not in the Northeast. It is obvious that Larry is not only a great teacher, but that his genetics have been passed on to the next generation. Now with the grandchildren such as Landon and another grandson, Johnny, developing into excellent deer hunters in their own right, there is little danger that the Benoit family deer hunting dynasty will fade away anytime soon.

If I were a young whitetail buck looking forward to the glorious ruts of the future, I would take that as very bad news indeed.

Chapter 2

Following Trophy Bucks

"Tracking isn't for everyone; it is incredibly demanding, both physically and mentally."

-Bryce M. Towsley

Standing in the rear are Larry (left) and Lanny Benoit; kneeling in front are Uncle Windy (left) and Mike Condon. Lanny guided Mike to this deer. Benoit photo.

If there is one certainty in modern deer hunting it is that the whitetail boom has made us poorer hunters. As technology brings us more and more products for hunting and the strategies we use become more homogenized, we are easing toward a generation of deer hunters who, while they may kill a lot of bucks, are without a lot of woods skills. As we become more and more detached from the dynamics of the woods we become merely interlopers there only to shoot a deer, as opposed to predators that are an active part of the cycle.

Certainly the almost universal use today of tree stands and blinds has made the masses more effective at harvesting deer, even while blunting our hunting skills. It is just not all that hard to find a place with lots of fresh deer sign or an active food source and to wait there for the deer to return. In doing so we exercise scouting more than hunting skills. Simply put, we "modern" hunters are effectively "ambushing" our deer while those highly refined woods skills needed for hunting styles more prevalent with past generations are left to rot in our memories.

Perhaps the purest form of whitetail hunting is tracking. To the uninformed it means simply that you find a deer track and follow it until you see and shoot the deer. In reality, it will call on almost every hunting skill available to man and it takes an overall woodsman with a profound understanding of whitetail behavior, coupled with exceptional woods skills, to succeed with any regularity. Trackers move through woods that are the deer's home. The deer live there every day of their lives, and survival dictates that they be sharp, smart, and wary. It is far easier to sit hidden in a tree and let a buck wander into range. There you are hidden from sight, you have no reason to move or make a sound. Your scent is controlled by your choice of location and the elevation. If you do it well, there is little reason for the buck to ever suspect you are in the area. Tracking, however, puts you on the ground and moving. You cannot control the variables nearly as well. It is impossible to move in most circumstances without making some sound, and as you travel where the track takes you, the wind can be blowing from any direction. Move-

Shane Benoit on the trail of a good buck. Bryce M. Towsley photo.

ment alone is often the giveaway, because deer and any other prey animal are by design tuned to movement. Their eyes are designed to see movement well and it is that which often keeps them from being eaten. Because of the evolution of the deer as a prey species, a moving hunter will find it far more difficult to remain undetected.

In short, if there is a tougher way to hunt whitetails than tracking, one that demands more skill, focus, and determination, I have yet to encounter it. Furthermore, in places that lend themselves well to this style of hunting, if there is a better way

Larry is fond of saying "The hardest part is finding a big buck. The easiest part is getting 'em out." He demonstrates that here. Benoit photo.

to consistently take trophy bucks, that too has eluded my notice.

Tracking is often considered "regional," and to some extent it is, because it is practiced extensively in the Northeast. It does work best in areas with snow, whitetail deer, and big expanses of land, which is a description of much of the far north in the eastern part of the country. The severe winters keep deer populations relatively low and huge areas of land are populated with only the deer that can survive in a much smaller winter habitat. In these big-country wilderness areas, deer densities are usually less than further south and there are often miles and miles of empty country between trophy bucks. The does will be found in "pockets" of habitat, and during the rut the bucks will be moving from one to another in search of a "love connection." Buck sign that was fresh yesterday could have been made by a deer that is now miles away, with no intention of returning. A tree stand hunter can be hunting truly fresh sign, but may never see the buck that left it behind. Stand hunting is a cold, lonely, and discouraging way to hunt these deer. Drives will not work in these huge expanses of land and are against the law in many places. Still hunting will have you wasting a lot of time in unproductive locations. When you boil it down, tracking is the most effective way to hunt that buck.

Tracking isn't for everyone; it is incredibly demanding, both physically and mentally. You must be able to walk for miles, all the while maintaining complete mental awareness. Often you will find yourself miles from camp or car when darkness falls, which means more walking, and you must be able to get up and do it again the next day, the one after that, and for as many days as it takes. You need complete comfort in the woods, without fear or even thoughts of getting lost, and when you finally shoot a buck, you may find yourself with a 250-pound deer and 6 miles of wilderness between you and the road.

It's work, heart wrenching, back breaking, discouraging work. But those who do it (and they are an increasingly smaller percentage of today's hunters) say there isn't a more effective way to kill a large, big-woods buck.

The question that begs to be asked is why, in today's world of deer hunting, a world that has proved the effectiveness of tree stands or blinds, a world that has moved away from tracking and hunting on the move as a hunting tactic, should you be interested in this book? You are not a tracker, you don't even live or hunt in a place where tracking is practiced, so what's in it for you?

Most will agree that the tracker is indeed a master of all of those forgotten woods skills, skills that in many of us have atrophied from lack of use, and few will dispute that the Benoits are the best trackers in the world. If we can also agree that tracking is the most demanding way to take trophy whitetail bucks and that it is a style that utilizes every hunting skill, then it could be strongly argued that they are also the best deer hunters in the world. Any hunter would be well advised to listen to what the Benoits have to say about deer hunting. Their advice will help you to be a better hunter, no matter what style you embrace. There is something here for every hunter. The more you learn about trophy buck behavior, reading sign, and finding big bucks, the better the hunter you will become. This deals with all whitetail bucks in any place they live, regardless of the possibility of snow or the density of deer populations. You may wish to use this knowledge to help place a tree stand, plan a drive, select a rattling location, or you may decide to give tracking a try. Regardless of your method, you better your chances for tagging the biggest buck of your life.

For years rumors have been bandied about that the Benoits "run down their bucks," that is that they simply chase them until the bucks can't run any more. Time and again I have been told by people who claimed to have the inside track that the Benoits camp on the trail, spending each night in the woods, and that they stay with the buck all day

Larry Benoit on a buck's track, 1997. Bryce M. Towsley photo.

long, often at a trot, until they kill him. It is usually considered that the only true skill they need is stamina and that, other than following the track until the deer wears out, is all that is necessary. "Of course," holds the conventional thinking, "not everybody is tough enough to hunt this way, so the Benoit methods are useless for most hunters."

"Baloney," said Larry Benoit. "I have never spent the night on a buck's trail and I don't spend much time running after them. It is a lot more in knowing how to read sign and being able to tell what that buck is going to do than it is about stamina. Sure you have to be in shape to track deer, but anybody can do it. It is a lot more important that you interpret the sign correctly and that you react to what it is telling you.

The author with a good buck from Alberta. Tracking can work any place there is snow. Bryce M. Towsley photo.

"It is also as much about being able to go slow; most hunters blow it at the end. You need to be able to read the sign and know what that buck is going to do. Sooner or later that buck is going to stop, he is likely worn out from rutting and chasing does and he wants a nap. Anybody can follow an easy track to that buck, but it takes a lot more to kill him. If you don't have the hunting skills to know when to slow down and how to slip up quietly, you will never get him. Killing trophy whitetails by tracking has a lot more to do with good hunting than it does with the ability to run up and down mountains."

It is also notable that tracking and the skills learned in tracking can apply in one form or another to any place deer are hunted—perhaps not always in the traditional sense, but some aspects of tracking will apply. In some parts of the Southwest and in Mexico, deer (usually mule deer) are tracked for long distances in the sand. The hunt has many similarities with tracking on snow, including the huge bucks that often are the end result. In the Southeast, it is not uncommon for the best bucks to prowl the fields for does and nourishment only to leave them before dawn to spend the day hiding in the thick woods. If conditions are right (such as a heavy dew or a light rain), a good tracker may be able to follow him to his lair and possess the skills to kill him there.

But more important is that tree stand hunters, or any other hunter, will learn from this book as well. The scouting and hunting techniques that the Benoits use will often pinpoint stand locations and will help to identify the quality of the buck you are hunting. The same applies to rattling. Finding likely places to call from, places that hold big bucks, makes more sense than just wandering and calling randomly. If you drive deer, it is always better to drive a patch of woods that you know has a good buck in it than to just randomly hope to find a deer.

Learning to read sign is important to any deer hunter. Are the big tracks you located from a buck or simply a big doe? Is it a young buck or an old mossy horn? What was he doing when he made those tracks? Is this a place he will return to or was he simply passing through? If this is a place he will come back to, when is he likely to return? What about weather? Can it influence when and if the buck will be back? How does the rut affect the buck's behavior? What about does in the area? Can you identify them and use them to your advantage?

Any deer hunter can benefit from learning the skills to move through the woods with confidence and stealth. No matter if you are slipping into your tree stand location or slipping up on a bedded buck, the less you alert the deer to your presence the higher your success rate. This is even more important with big, dominant trophy bucks because they simply will not tolerate a lot of human activity. It is easy to chase a smart old buck out of the ar-

ea, or force him to go nocturnal. Sometimes one mistake is all it takes.

Trackers compete on the deer's turf. They pit their inferior senses against the deer's far better hearing and sense of smell. The only advantage trackers have are their brains. But that advantage must be applied to the senses that they still rely on. Trackers must use their brains to know when to look for the deer and then tell their eyes to look harder, look more, look better and to spot the buck before he bolts. You must be able to spot deer in the woods if you have any hope of success. Many hunters today look for movement, but if trackers do this it is already too late; they must learn to look for the deer, a skill that will help any hunter's success rate.

Shane shooting at a buck. Bryce M. Towsley photo.

Shots while tracking tend to be fleeting and rare. This style of hunting calls for good shooting skills, including getting the shot off fast. Waiting for a "better shot" is bad strategy because often there isn't one. Shooting skills that allow you to shoot quickly and with confidence are beneficial to any hunter who uses a gun.

Any hunter who can and will penetrate deeper into the woods is likely to find more deer, less spooky deer, and usually bigger bucks. It's a simple fact of life that deer will move away from human activity, and humans often don't like to venture too far into the woods. Except trackers—they go where the track leads them. The skills that take them deep into the wilderness and back with ease and comfort will aid any hunting style in accessing the bucks that are back away from the crowds.

Don't make the mistake of thinking that if you are not and do not want to be a tracker that there is nothing in this book for you. Any serious trophy whitetail hunter will learn from what the Benoits have to teach. While you may never actually track a buck for miles and miles as they do, you will without a doubt put to use the skills and techniques that are presented in this book.

Chapter 3

Footprints in the Snow

"I told you, it's a good place to hunt!"

-A hunter explaining why he keeps hunting the same deer-free place year after year.

It's a simple fact that most hunters do not kill big, dominant, trophy bucks because they fail to hunt where those bucks are. Just hunting in a state or even a given area that produces big deer is not enough—you must hunt in the exact places those deer live, travel, feed, and breed.

Several years ago a friend invited me to hunt with him on some family property in the Northeast Kingdom of Vermont. Year after year this vast unsettled area of my home state produces the majority of the 200-pound plus deer taken in the state, and I was excited about the prospects. He raved about the big 8-point buck his brother had taken

there (many years earlier as it turned out) and about how it was "a great place to hunt." I knew he wasn't a particularly avid hunter, but his enthusiasm about this place was contagious.

I arrived with my Uncle Butch well before daylight to meet my friend and his brother. A fresh snow had fallen during the night and conditions couldn't have been better. As we finished the last of our coffee and prepared to start hunting, my friend again remarked about how this was "a good place to hunt."

At dark I arrived back at the truck tired, wet, and quite discouraged. I had not seen a deer track all

A lone tracker in Vermont's Northeast Kingdom. Bryce M. Towsley photo.

day. I mentioned this and all three of the other hunters reported pretty much the same luck.

"In fact," said my buddy, "we haven't seen a deer all season."

A bit peeved, but trying hard not to show it, I asked why they kept coming back to this place. In a stretch of Yankee logic my buddy replied, "I told you, it's a good place to hunt!"

It is easy to get into a habit of hunting the same place year after year. Perhaps you or your partners have taken deer there in the past, or maybe it's just where you have always hunted, but it can cost you big bucks. Land is never stagnant, trees grow or are cut down, habitat changes, and the deer can move on.

Most places that trophy deer are hunted fit with the old saying that "even when there are lots of them, there ain't many." This is never truer than in the vast unsettled stretches of the north country; there just aren't all that many true trophy bucks when compared to the amount of country.

This leads to another trap many hunters fall into when they tend to think too small in terms of hunting areas. This may be fine in farm areas or on land that is well managed for high deer numbers, but when you are hunting in the northern forest, thinking small is a huge mistake. Like Larry says, "you can't just go out in the back yard and start walking." If you are in a big area, such as in northern Maine, you may cover 50, 60, or 100 miles by truck before you locate a good buck."

The huge tracts of land there will never hold many deer, and those that are present will often be found in pockets of habitat with miles and miles of virtually empty land in between. The "pockets" of

Typical hunting habitat in Maine. Bucks will often travel the line at the bottom of the spruce where they meet the old clear-cut, about one-third of the way up the mountain. Bryce M. Towsley photo.

deer are fluid and may change with changing conditions. This is especially true during the hunting season when weather and feed are in a constant state of flux and hunting pressure comes into play. The empty land will often contain tracks or other deer sign, made by deer that were passing through or perhaps even living there for a while before moving on to a different location. Hunters who are fooled into hunting here are in for a disappointment. You must be able to read the sign and determine if the deer are still hanging around, have moved on, or were just passing though. Locating the current hideout of the does, where they are feeding, and where they are bedding is important to finding big bucks during the rut.

The determining factor on the number of deer in most northern latitudes is the winter habitat, which is only a small percentage of the land, but is crucial to how many deer survive each year to populate the rest of the land. With the severe winters in these northern locations, the amount and quality of winter habitat generally keeps deer per square mile densities relatively low.

Because deer are social animals, they will congregate into groups, usually in places that contain the right mixture of cover and food. These "pockets" of deer will contain does, fawns, and young bucks. The older, dominant bucks tend to be grumpy loners who spend most of their time far from these social and family groups. The exception comes during the rut when these surly old bucks will forsake their hermit's existence to search out these groups of deer, looking for does to breed. A buck will wander far and wide during this time and will often let his cautious nature be overridden by his intense desire to breed. In doing this he is letting his defenses down, and that makes him vulnerable.

Bucks are ready for action long before the majority of does are ready to breed and will spend a lot of time wandering and looking. Furthermore, most trophy bucks don't harbor a lot of what many consider "family values," and monogamy is not their strong suit. When a doe is bred and no longer interested, the buck is gone and in search of another hot doe. They will continue this from long before the first doe comes into heat until long after the last one in their neighborhood has been bred. They will cover miles and miles of land in their frustrating search and leave lots of tracks behind.

Concentrating your search for trophy deer in places that are known to attract bucks is always a good idea. Lanny looks for swamps or mountain ranges, particularly mountains with thick vegetation on the top. He says that, "High on the mountains you won't find a lot of deer, but sooner or later you will find a pocket of deer and there might be a good buck track in there."

Shane looks for what they call "shitholes," a colloquial term that describes the thickest, most

Larry (left) and Shane check out the tracks of a big buck that crossed the road just before daylight. Bryce M. Towsley photo.

tangled up mess of vegetation, blowdowns, and trees in an area.

Larry looks for the hardest country he can find, places where no other hunters want to venture. "The harder the country, the better," he says. "There are not too many people willing to work that hard and the bucks know it."

They all agree that big bucks are loners with predictable habits and many will have their favorite spots they keep going back to again and again. You don't necessarily have to go into these places. The chances of actually killing the buck in there are not good; after all that's why he chose the spot in the first place. But, knowing and recognizing them as a buck's hangout is the key to finding the home of a trophy buck. He may be in there resting and recuperating from several nights of chasing does, but he won't stay for long. Think about it: deer breed only once a year and for a very short time span. If you were a healthy male who only got lucky a few weeks a year, how much time would you spend hanging around home during those weeks? Sooner or later the buck will leave and start traveling in search of hot does. When he does he has to leave tracks, but you have to know where to look.

One very good way to locate a buck during this time is to cruise the back roads, watching carefully for places where a buck has crossed.

"Sometimes if the conditions are right I'll spend most of the day cruising the logging roads locating

Personalized art adorns Shane's rifle. Also shown is a set of antlers from one of the many deer the rifle has taken. Bryce M. Towsley photo.

big buck tracks," Lanny Benoit told me. "It is a great way to get a handle on travel routes and on what areas hold trophy bucks."

It is not unusual to rack up a few hundred miles on the logging roads when scouting. Even when hunting, simply locating a track is not a guarantee that the Benoits will follow it. Shane says that a lot of times they will locate several tracks before deciding which one to hunt. If the conditions are right, they will be out well before daylight looking for places where a big buck has crossed the road. As each track is located and identified as a buck worthy of hunting, they also will try to age the track to have an idea of when it was made and to help in guessing where the buck might be currently. (Identifying and aging tracks is covered in detail in Chapter 4.) Then they make a mental note of its location and keep moving. Sometimes they will already know and recognize identifying characteristics of the buck because often they will see the track of the same buck at more than one location. This helps to work out where his travel route is taking him and where he might be at any given time. As a pattern emerges they will use it to plan the strategy for hunting this buck. Bucks travel in circles, or "swings" as the Benoits call them, and if you can understand and predict that cycle it can help you identify where the buck may be at a given time.

If they catch a big buck entering into a block of woods and they circle that block without finding that he has exited, that gives them a starting point. Often, too, if the section of woods has a high mountain with thick spruce cover on top, they have a good idea that the buck is bedded for the day. Big bucks tend to favor these locations to bed down and rest from the night's activities. This is a big advantage for the hunter because the buck is stationary, which allows the hunter time to gain ground on his track. This is a good situation, and the track is a likely candidate to follow.

Knowing and understanding what the buck is doing and where he might be is important before committing to following the track. A track that was left sometime in the night by a buck on the move may go for miles as that buck wanders in his quest for friendly does. That buck may well be bedded down during the daylight hours, but it may be a long way from where you find his tracks. A hunter can spend all day following him and never catch up. Yet if you know or at least can make an educated guess that the track was made recently and that the buck has likely bedded down, there is a far better chance of catching up with that deer.

Shane sums it up well when he says that, "It's best to pick a buck who is at the end of his night's journey and ready to lie down for a while. Your chances are far better for killing him." Of course the trick is in knowing if he is indeed at the end of his journey or if he is full of energy and determined to walk all day.

This is where it is important to know deer behavior and the habitat of the areas. If the track is coming down off a big spruce-covered mountain top or out of a dense swamp, chances are that the buck is leaving his bedding area and is rested and ready for a romp. You may get behind this buck and walk your legs to stubs without ever seeing him. Don't forget he has four legs and you have two. He lives all year in these woods and is in the best physical shape of his life, while you probably spent most of the last nine months in a chair. Don't think you can out-walk him, because you can't. However, if that track is leading into (rather than out of) these places, particularly if it was made in the last hours of darkness or first hours of daylight, that deer may well be worn out and ready for bed. This is a buck you may have a chance of tagging. The point is to pick your battles. Find a buck you have a chance to kill. Don't follow a track just because it is there and it is big. Make sure it is also reasonable to think you can catch the deer.

Make sure, too, that you have at least a general idea of when the track was made. If it is very old that doesn't necessarily mean it is not a candidate to follow. If the buck is bedded or better still with a hot doe, even a track many hours old can take you to him relatively soon. If the deer is not covering much ground you can make up the time. But if the track is old and the deer is wandering, forget it, go find another buck.

Shane and I were out looking for tracks on a Sunday when hunting is not allowed in Maine. We found where two bucks were following a doe who was just coming into heat. Obviously she wasn't ready to breed, but with deer "no" doesn't necessarily mean "no," and these bucks were hounding her unmercifully. She was running, as was indicated by her splayed feet, while the bucks were plodding along behind.

"My guess is that she headed into the thick stuff to get rid of them," Shane said. "Bucks have trouble getting through the really thick stuff. Their racks hang up on the brush and of course they are simply bigger than the does. The does know that and use it to their advantage when they are not yet ready to breed. If this was a hunting day I'll bet we could head down into the slash in that old clear-cut and find those bucks."

Later that same morning we found where a big buck had been walking down the road. It had stopped snowing just before daylight, and these tracks were clear and fresh, so we knew when they were made. He suddenly turned and ran off, throwing up gravel and digging the road. He was obviously spooked, probably from a vehicle coming along right after daylight. Shane looked up at the spruce-covered mountain top that the tracks headed for and sighed.

"This buck is up there bedded. We could get him in a couple of hours. If we could only hunt."

In places that experience even moderate hunting pressure the bucks will soon become vehicle wise. One unfortunate sidebar to their notoriety is that anyplace the Benoits hunt will soon enough have more hunting pressure. Lots of hunters will follow them around, and while many will not leave the roads, they do increase the traffic in the area. That doesn't mean that there are trucks every few yards, because in these remote places a few trucks a day can be a lot. The bucks are used to little or no traffic and they recognize that the extra vehicles every

day means something, most likely danger. Many bucks react by avoiding the roads. They will not cross them much in daylight and it is not unusual for them to be bedded just off the edge a few hundred yards, lying there watching the traffic. This can make it hard to find fresh tracks by driving the logging roads. Often, though, getting out and walking through likely places will show you a lot of tracks near roads that would have you believing there wasn't a buck in miles.

This buck was walking down the road when something, perhaps a vehicle, spooked it. If it was a hunter, it was likely sometime close to dawn, so this is a good track to follow. Bryce M. Towsley photo.

Last year Lanny ran a buck all over a mountain, but it would not cross or come near to the road. He finally killed the deer late in the day. Three days later day he and Landon tracked a buck that went around the same area several times, but didn't want to cross the road. There was probably a doe in heat there that was attracting all of the bucks and certainly she was contributing to his reluctance to leave that patch of woods, but being road smart had a lot to do with it as well. Bucks and most other animals will travel in circles when pushed, and in this case he simply made smaller circles to avoid crossing any roads.

The snow was frozen and crunchy. The buck could hear them walking and stayed just ahead of the hunt-

Shane Benoit. Bryce M. Towsley photo.

ers. At times he was so close that Lanny could hear the buck walking, but they didn't get a look.

Larry points out that, "a big dominant buck is not going to have just a couple of miles swing in his travels. He will eat a lot of ground during his nightly walk. Many hunters don't realize just how far they can travel and they start following the track the first place they see it, never catching up with the deer. You can't out-walk him, so you have to out-think him. Use the tools you have to figure out where he is going, then find his tracks close to there and follow them."

The weather plays a big part in how, if, or for how long you might ride the roads locating tracks.

"One thing I know for certain," said Lanny, "is that big bucks move a lot less before a storm. It is not uncommon to find almost no big buck tracks before a storm. The bucks are just not moving, except to feed a little. They will lie down, get up, feed, lie down, but they don't cover much ground. They know when a big storm's coming and they are not going to get caught unprepared. You may see does, skippers [fawns], and even small bucks during this time, but you will not likely find big tracks. You won't find big buck tracks around the does and you will see few big footprints cutting across the high ground or crossing roads. They just are not moving.

"If you want to find the bucks then, they are usually up high on the mountain in the thick spruce on top," Lanny continues. "I have often found three or four beds where they stayed until the storm came and then waited it out. A day or so after the storm they are back on the move. That's the time to check out your hunting territory in long wide sweeps. If you are on foot, watch the funnel areas or the high points of roads. A buck almost always will cross at the height of the land and will stop to look around there. This is a great place to locate tracks. If you are a stand hunter it is a good place to wait as well.

"If you have a foot of snow, you will change the way you are going to hunt. In the morning if you have new snow and the storm is over you are going to ride the roads looking for a big buck track. The deer will be on the move and you might ride 3 or 4 hours before going in the woods. But when you do, chances are it will be on a buck track that is fresh and you will have a good chance to kill that deer.

"On days like this I'll be up at 3:00 or 3:30 in the morning and ready to start looking for tracks. This is particularly true on overcast or dark nights because these nights will have more deer traveling. Regardless of what conventional wisdom says, the deer move less during a full moon night. I have kept track of this through the years and am absolutely sure that a dark night is better for movement. On a cold, clear night the deer don't move much, not like a damp and overcast night when it seems that every deer in the woods is on the move.

"During the rut bucks move when they are rested up and not too tired to go. If they are all beat to hell from breeding does, fighting other bucks, and traveling, they will lie down. They will go up high on the mountain or else down low in a swamp and rest, sometimes for a day or two.

"Have you ever heard about somebody tracking a buck and all the deer wanted to do was lie down? That's because he is all tired out from chasing does and he wants to rest. He's got to lie down, he is worn out and he just can't go any more."

"It's not too bad a situation for the hunter as long as the deer are not too spooky," Lanny continued. "But, I don't really like them lying down. I would rather have them up, moving, not paying attention, and looking for does. As we get older of course it's not as easy to travel as much ground, so the bedded buck helps there, but if they are up and looking for does it's easier to come up on them undetected than if they are lying down.

"Now I have shot a bunch lying down, but the ideal set up is a fresh, brand new track of a buck that has just left his bed. The only thing he's got on his mind now is finding a doe. He's easier to get because he is curious, he is smelling every track, hooking trees, and not paying attention. He doesn't care about anything but sex and all he wants to do is look for does. When he is lying down trying to get some sleep he will spot you coming up on him, because he's looking. But, when he's pawing the ground or hooking trees he's not paying attention.

"Sometimes a bedded buck hears you coming and may even think you are a doe. Then you have a chance, but it's tough because that deer is watching and is alert to your presence. With the deer moving, sometimes you will catch him in the open hardwoods. You may work it right so that you come up over one rise and catch him going over the next one. Then you have him.

"If a deer is not too spooky and is thinking about does it's not all that important to kill him the first time you see him. If he has breeding on his mind, he will forget all about you. You can even sometimes shoot at him and miss and he will not spook too bad. More than once I have been so tuckered out that I was breathing hard and I missed, but the bucks didn't spook too bad and gave me another chance 5 minutes, a half hour, or a even a couple of hours later. I guess that is proof that it's always best to rest the gun against a tree, but sometimes you just don't have that option.

"One time I was close to a buck that kept lying down, it was thick and I couldn't see him. I was sneaking up over the hummocks and spotted his head peeking over the next one and looking back at me. He could see me before I could see him and I didn't get him, at least not that time. He wanted very badly to lie down. He kept waiting for me, and I knew that eventually it would cost him.

"On the other hand, if the buck is spooky and not thinking about does it's a good thing to kill him the first time you see him or it can get real tough. He will know you are behind him, he is concentrating on staying alive rather than on breeding, and a smart old buck in this situation can make it real hard to put a tag in his ear."

When tracks are hard to find, Larry likes to stay up high on the mountains. He says, "Look for bedded bucks before, after, and during a storm. Try to jump them up in the thick spruce on top or near the top of the mountains. If the bucks are holding tight and not moving and there are no tracks, you have to make them move. Walk in a zigzag course near the mountain top and you will likely see bucks.

"You must anticipate where and when you will find a buck. If you are to have any chance at all of

killing him the first time you see him you must have everything out of your mind. Anticipate you will see a big buck and sooner or later you will see him, but one or two bounds and he will be gone, so you have to be ready. He may be anywhere, you can't know where he is so you need to keep looking. Separate human thinking and animal thinking. Deer don't think like a man, and to be successful you must train yourself to think like a deer. Years of experience is the only real way to do this, but you must be concentrating on finding the deer and that alone. You can't be thinking about getting lost or if you left lights on in the car, how you are going to pay this month's bills or anything else except

Using a map to help plot buck movement is helpful for most hunters. Shown is John Kascenska, the author's father-in-law. Bryce M. Towsley photo.

finding that deer. You have to concentrate and not let your mind wander. The second you let your guard down is when you will see him and he will get away. That's a guarantee."

In saying that most hunters will think too small about their hunting areas, that means much too small. Even in big country we tend to concentrate on far too small an area. The Benoits hunt throughout hundreds of square miles of Maine wilderness. Much of their time is spent in learning the layout of the land, which roads are on the far side of the mountains, where they go, and where they come from. They don't use maps, and Shane says he prefers to keep it all in his head.

"If the information is in your head you won't lose it or leave it behind like you can a map," he says. "And you can't leave it around for somebody to find and steal your hard work like you can with a map."

While they can rely on sharp memories, most of us are not blessed with that kind of retention and would be well advised to carry and use maps of their areas. The Benoits are always learning more territory and they advise any hunter to spend some time scouting before or during the deer season. Mark your map with places you have seen big buck sign, both while scouting and hunting. Also note where you are finding concentrations of does, particularly during the hunting season, then leave them alone. In the northern latitudes a majority of does are bred within just a few days of each other. With the buck-to-doe ratios common to these areas, that means a lot of does for each dominant buck to breed. When this happens, and he has collected a harem, he stops wandering. When the buck finds receptive does in estrus and ready to breed, or those who are about to become receptive, he will likely stay with these deer until he has bred any and all that are in estrus or until he is run off by a larger buck.

During this period Shane says, "Look where the does are hanging around, but don't mess with them. Leave them alone and instead circle to check if a big buck has moved in to where they are. Keep circling to see if he has left, and if not, then try tracking in after him.

"I was doing this with a good buck one time and his track kept going in and out of this little pocket of does. I kept working along the edge, far enough out so I wouldn't spook any deer. I was trying to find his track to see if he had left when a doe came running out. I knew I hadn't spooked her so I waited. When does aren't quite yet ready to breed they will run away from the bucks, but the bucks can tell they are getting close and they keep after them. Ten minutes later he came plodding along her track and I got him. He was a good 10-pointer that weighed 205 pounds.

"Does that have food, water, and shelter will not usually leave the area unless hunters push them out. Leave them alone because sooner or later a big buck will come along to check them out. There are small bucks with the does. Leave them alone too, you are not here to shoot these small bucks and if you insist on getting a look at them you will eventually spook them and likely the does as well."

The inclination for many hunters is to go in and hunt around the does in hopes of running into a buck. However, if you alert the does to your presence you can actually chase them or any big bucks out of the area. There are too many eyes, ears, and noses around to think you can get away with poking around with the deer hoping to see a buck. The first time you spook a doe and it goes charging off, crashing brush, and snorting, any big buck in the area will know what's happening. The only thing you will see of him is the tracks he left behind when he vacated the area.

Shane with a 205-pound, 10-point buck he shot in 1995. Benoit photo.

Shane continues, "If you know the locations of deer concentrations and the rut is on, it is better to circle the area and look for big buck tracks leading in or out of the doe's core areas. If you find a track, unless it is smoking hot, don't follow it right off. Instead, complete your circle. Remember that these areas can be big, so make sure your circle is large enough to allow for the entire area the does are using. If a track is leading into the doe's area, but fails to come out, you know he is in there somewhere. If you find where he exited the area, then you are already on a fresher track and have saved time in trying to sort out his night's activities in chasing does.

"If you have a hot track and you know it is a trophy buck you can follow it, but it won't be easy. The buck will often be crazy with lust if there is a ready doe and he will sometimes let you get away with making a mistake, but don't count on it. There will almost always be other deer, or even several, with him and usually there is a satellite buck or two around that he is busy keeping away from his does. Often there will be lots and lots of tracks where this buck and his rivals have chased the doe or does around and it will be hard to sort out. You can easily find yourself looking far too much at the ground and not paying attention to what's going on.

"The up side is that you can just as easily run into a satellite buck that is a trophy. Just because he is not the dominant buck doesn't mean he isn't a shooter. A 275-pound buck may be bullying the others from breeding, but if those smaller bucks are 230 pounds, that's usually fine with most hunters.

"Sometimes, too, you may be on the track of a good buck only to cross the trail of an even better buck. A doe in heat is like a magnet and will suck in any buck in the area and anything can happen."

According to Larry, "Often you will be on a good track and you will come on another bigger or fresher track. You may want to leave the first track for the second. That first one isn't going anywhere—so let's try this one for a change, we can always come back to the first one. Of course we have done that and wound up not getting any of them!"

You have to adapt to the situation as well. Larry gives an example in a buck that Shane shot.

"One time we had been keeping an eye on some does for several days and late one afternoon we found that a big buck had moved in there. The next morning we found four or five guys in there ahead of us and after the buck. These guys were making too much noise and we knew that the buck would move on out of there to escape them. There was a long swamp that ran parallel to the road for miles and we thought that the buck would stay in it for the cover it provided. We were pretty sure he would avoid the open hardwoods on the other side of the swamp and since we never cut a track along the road, we knew he was still in the swamp. We kept checking for his tracks along the logging roads that crossed the swamp, finding them at each location. About 8 miles down Shane got out and started up a perpendicular logging road and hit his track. This time the track looked pretty fresh so he started after him. Before he had gone too far he found where the buck had rubbed a tree and then picked up a doe, so he knew that he was no longer fleeing and that he felt safe about the distance he had between the other hunters and himself. He continued to follow him to a clear-cut where he could see their tracks crossing. On the other side there was a line of cedars where he thought they would bed or at least stop to rest. As he came up to the cedars he knew that it was so thick he would have a problem with seeing the buck in time enough to shoot him. Finally he came to a stump. Knowing he was close, he jumped up on the stump with his rifle ready. As soon as he did the doe started blowing and took off with the buck right behind her. Shane shot several times at the buck before losing sight of him. Then he saw the doe cross a clearing, but the buck wasn't with her. He knew then that one of two things had happened, either he got him or the buck had cut off from the doe and was 'getting out of Dodge.'" A short walk gave him the answer.

He had 11 points and weighed 268 pounds dressed.

Chapter 4

Reading, Identifying, and Understanding Tracks

"Teaching somebody to read sign is a lot like telling them how to read a book. We can teach you to read, but you have to read some books before you really know how. There is a lot that you can't put into words, we can get you started, but experience and common sense will give you the rest."

-Lanny Benoit

"Know what's on the ground."

-Larry Benoit

It may well be the most asked question at the deer hunting seminars that the Benoits conduct, "How can you be sure you are on the track of a big buck?" Perhaps no single segment of tracking deer is harder to teach than this. Identifying big buck tracks is tougher than you might think, and teaching somebody else how to do it definitely is.

Tracking is gut-wrenchingly hard work. It is undoubtedly the most physically demanding of all of the whitetail deer hunting methods. It can wear you down and wear you out. It can reduce the toughest of hunters to tears and frustrate the most patient. To put forth that degree of effort for anything less than a big mature buck is foolish and a bit masochistic. Identifying the track you plan to follow as that of a trophy buck is important, very important, and very difficult.

Certainly size does count—there are just not that many 300-pound does running around in any woods. If the track is grossly larger than any other deer tracks in the area and you are certain you are not looking at a moose's Nike print, the chances are

Left to right: 268 pounds (Shane), 268 pounds (Lanny), and 263 pounds (Lane) from 1991. Shane Benoit photo.

better than ever that it's a big buck and you can pursue it in good faith.

The facts are, though, that most trophy bucks, regardless of the region, are a lot closer to 200 pounds than they are to 300 pounds, and it is not totally unheard of for an old northern doe to have a track nearly as large as these more common specimens. You must learn to look at the total message the deer is leaving you. Simply finding a big track is not always enough.

"One time we stopped to look at big track in the road," Shane told me in that quiet, confident way that is uniquely his. "I walked a little way down over the bank looking at the track and then jumped back in the rig and said 'Come on Pop, let's go, it's nothing I want.'

"Another guy we know came along later and saw where we stopped to look at the track. He thought it was big enough that it had to be a good buck and he decided to follow it. He trailed that deer all day, catching up to it just before dark. It turned out to be a big-footed doe. We saw him later and he told me about it, saying, 'Now I know why you didn't follow it.'

"When I followed her the little bit after she crossed the road she went through a bunch of trees that were all tangled up and brushy, then I saw where she went between a couple of trees that were very close together. I thought there is something weird about this track, it was made by a big deer with a big foot for sure, but it can't have much of a rack. That's why I decided to pass. I didn't know for sure if it was a doe, but I did know it was nothing I wanted to hunt."

And of course even the Benoits can make the wrong decision now and then. Larry tells of one time when that was the case...well sort of. "We like big-bodied bucks and we know what we are looking for," he said. "Another guy might pass it by without noticing or knowing what he is seeing, but we will see it and understand. We want big 200-pound or better bucks and that's what we look for in a track.

"One time we passed the same track time and time again over the course of several days. Shane

and I saw it, Lanny saw it too, but it wasn't appealing to us. We knew it was a buck, but it wasn't all that big so we decided to leave him alone. We sicced another guy, a friend of ours, on him and he tracked that deer down and killed him. He had a huge rack! He wasn't very big in body size, but he was more than 20 inches wide with 10 long points. If we had followed him we would have realized he had a good rack and would have gone after him, but his small track turned us off.

The track from Shane's 268-pound, tight-racked buck. Note the wide spacing and long stride and how he walks flat-footed. Benoit photo.

"Of course, on the other hand, sometimes a 200-pound plus buck might not have much of a rack on him. But, what we really like is the big body weights of these northern deer, so that's what we look for more than the rack."

Lanny makes a point when he says that, "A good tracker can tell if it is a deer worthy of taking within a short distance, sometimes as little as 100 feet, but almost always in a 1/4 mile. You have to see the entire picture, not just the individual tracks. Look at the stride, the distance between the left and right legs, and how the deer walks. A lot of hunters look for drag marks, but drag marks don't matter. All deer drag their feet, particularly if the snow is more

Notice the way this buck's urine is scattered over a wider area than the neat little spots left by does. Bryce M. Towsley photo.

than a couple of inches deep. Buck do it more than does, but it's hard to tell which is which from that alone. A buck swaggers more, has a wider chest so the tracks are farther apart, and that is one of the best indicators of how big a buck you are after. A track that is wide spaced will be made by a wide-bodied deer; that usually means a good buck. It is sort of like the difference between how a football player and a cheerleader walk. They are not only built differently, but they have different attitudes that show up in their walks. A trophy buck's stance is wider because he is bigger, but he also swaggers like a big-chested football player when he walks, where a doe keeps her feet in line in a more dainty 'ladylike' manner."

Another good indicator of a big buck is the length of his stride. A good buck will tend to have a much longer body and longer legs than a smaller deer. This will show up in the length of his stride.

A buck may rub trees and make scrapes as he travels along and that is as sure a sign as you can receive. Also, a doe will travel through and under brush that a big buck has to go around to avoid tangling his antlers.

Another clue is that a buck may urinate as he walks along, making dribble marks in the snow like an incontinent old fool. He is marking territory similar to how a dog will and he will urinate on most of the other deer tracks he crosses. He may leave urine marks in the snow as much as 5 feet long, whereas a doe will usually squat and go in one place.

Even when a buck is simply relieving himself it will look a lot different than when a doe does it. A doe will leave a nice neat hole in the snow that is concentrated in a relatively small place. The mark in the snow will be behind or centered on her tracks. A buck will urinate in front of his tracks. Also, because his penis is loose and hanging down from his body, it will wobble around like a hose that nobody has hold of and dribble over a larger area. That area is not as large as lots of hunters might think; some are looking for a square yard when in reality it is only a few inches. However, the area of the urine stain

This is the track of a big buck. Note the width between the tracks and the long stride. As far as anybody knows, this buck is still alive. Benoit photo.

Tracks from Shane's 1995 205-pound, 10-point buck. Benoit photo.

from a buck will be about twice or more in size than that of a doe's. Sometimes, too, a buck will walk along a little as he is urinating, spreading the stain over still a larger area. Often when he is stepping over a log, particularly one with snow on it, he will leave a small urine stain. A buck may also urinate down his hind legs and over his hocks, usually when he is making a scrape.

A buck in rut is a raunchy fellow and his urine will have a strong and definitive odor to it, smelling much stronger than a doe's urine, particularly a doe that is not in heat.

The buck's track passed through these two trees, indicating that his antlers were at least narrower than the trees. Because he had avoided narrower trees earlier on, we have a good indication of his antlers' width. Bryce M. Towsley photo.

Watch how the deer moves through the brush, how he picks his route, and how he places his feet. A buck with a large rack is going to go around places that he may have trouble getting his rack through, such as thick brush or trees that grow closely together. This is particularly true when he is not in a hurry or spooked in any way. An overhanging branch that is side-stepped for no apparent reason can be an indication of a good-racked buck.

I was hunting with Shane last fall when he showed me several examples of this. One was two trees spaced about 18 inches apart. The buck we were on deliberately stepped out of the obvious path that would have taken him between those trees and walked around them. He then stepped back into the trail he was on and continued. Also, we saw several locations where he had to "step around" lone trees close to the trail. Once Shane pointed it out to me I could plainly see how the buck stepped to the side of his path to ease around the tree.

"Why doesn't he just move his head to the side as he passed the tree, rather than step around?" I asked.

"I can't say for sure," replied Shane, "but they prefer to step around. I suppose it is something that is ingrained into their brain from when their antlers are in velvet and subject to easy damage. Perhaps, too, as the rut continues and they develop those huge neck muscles they get a little muscle bound and it is easier to step around the tree than to swing their neck. Regardless of the reason, it is one of the very best indicators of whether or not the buck you are following has a wide rack. They will push through small brush and whips, but anything an inch or more in diameter they will go around."

As Lanny points out, though, they can put their antlers through something much narrower than the width of the antlers. Sometimes they will tip or twist their heads to get through the brush. It is just as important to look for how a buck steps through brush or a tight squeeze between trees, where one foot will usually be off to one side as he steps to work his rack through. Subtle little signs like this make a huge difference in interpreting the tracks you are following.

He also points out that sometimes you can be fooled, "Pop shot a real good buck a few years back whose rack went almost straight up. He didn't act like a wide-racked trophy buck because he wasn't, but he turned out to have a great set of horns."

In 1991 Shane took a buck that he knew had a "tight" rack a long time before he ever saw it. While tracking the deer he found where it had rubbed a large tree and he knew that even though it was a trophy buck it had an unusual rack because the deer couldn't get his antlers around the tree he was rubbing. It almost looked like a spike buck was rubbing the tree because all he could do was run his tines up and down the bark. But of course, the other sign told the tale that he was a large mature buck. When he finally shot the deer, he found that the main beams came around and almost touched in the front.

Another way to judge the trophy quality of a deer's antlers is to look at where the buck has put his nose into another deer's track or lowered his head to grab a bite of food. If you see marks made in the snow by his rack, you can often make a judgment on his size in addition to being sure that it's a buck's trail you are on.

One time when we were on the track of a good buck, Larry showed me a place where the buck had put his head down to grab some small, low-growing browse. The tips of his antlers had clearly defined themselves in the snow on either side of the spot he had fed. They measured 28 inches between them at the widest point. When I allowed for the lateral movement of his head as he fed, which was well indicated in the snow and the angle as he tipped his head, it looked like his antler spread from tip to tip was at least 20 to 22 inches. Sadly, we will never know for sure because it got dark before we caught up with that buck.

Larry points out that eventually any buck will feed, and when he does, if he is any good at all, you will almost always find an imprint of the rack in the snow. It might not be the front tines that stick in the snow, but the back ones, the G-3s, usually will. It can be hard to tell for sure, but usually you can get

The tree that Shane's 268-pound, 10-point buck rubbed (1991). Benoit photo.

This is a place where a buck put his head down to feed. Note the antler marks on either side, indicating a good buck. Bryce M. Towsley photo.

an idea of the spread. With a good imprint you can get an idea of how many points he has. If you see 3 points on each side you know you are likely after a 10-point buck, because the brow tines and main beams will usually not show.

A bedded buck will very often leave an imprint of one side of his antlers in the snow. A buck will lay out and put his head down to sleep, leaving an imprint of one side of his rack in the snow. Often he will be holding his head up, but will doze and lose control for a moment, like we do when we are trying to stay awake watching TV, and his rack will drop and hit the snow, leaving a sharp imprint of one side.

Larry was tracking a buck one time when he found where he had left a perfect imprint near his bed, showing that he had 7 points on that side. Larry told Lanny that night that he was after a 13 or 14-point buck. Five days later he finally shot the deer, which had a 13-point rack.

Larry likes to see a buck's bed in the snow. He says that it is one of the very best identifying clues that you are after a buck.

"Look for stains from tarsal glands in the bed," he says. "That is a sure sign of a buck. Does will leave stains from urine or, if they are in heat, they will be secreting fluids, but it always will be from their butt and will be located where that laid in their bed, near the edge. Bucks will have their belly stained from breeding and they will have been urinating down their legs and over their tarsal glands. His back legs will be under him, so either way the stains will be nearer the middle of the bed. It will also be yellow where he is lying because a buck's penis is under his belly and that area will be stained with urine and semen if he is rutting. You can even smell that in the bed. This is a good way to tell it was a buck that bedded there, put your nose down there and sniff! This works particularly well on bare-ground where you can't see the stains. A buck's bed will have a very identifiable odor."

Of course the track is the most common sign and is often the biggest indicator of what kind of deer you are after. Larry says that a big buck track will be as wide as a .30-06 shell.

"Lots of pictures that you see will show the shell in the length of the track, but that's wrong. Look for width more than length for a big buck track. It is the width that is the best indicator of how good a buck is. Lots of deer can have long feet, just like a teenaged boy may have feet too big for his body. But a big, heavy buck will be a big-boned deer. He will likely have long feet, but he will certainly have wide feet. Any track that is wider than a .30-06 or .270 shell is the track of a trophy buck. Also, look for width in dew claws. That too can indicate a big-boned, large-bodied deer. The dew claws on a doe or young buck will be spaced close together, but an older, big buck will have a larger bone structure that will have the dew claws spaced well apart.

"Just remember that the size of the foot is but one indicator," Larry cautioned. "You must look at the big picture. That includes how he walks. Little bucks tend to walk on their toes, where a big buck is more flat-footed. As bucks get older and bigger they tend to become more and more flat-

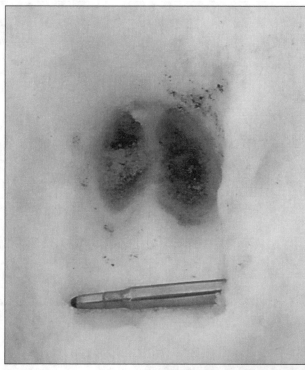

Most hunters will use a cartridge to gauge a track's size, but they often do it incorrectly. This buck's dew claws are as wide as a .30-06 cartridge, which indicates a big-boned buck. This is likely a good trophy weighing more than 200 pounds field dressed. Bryce M. Towsley photo.

This is a young buck, but he still may be a trophy. The cartridge is a .300 Weatherby. Bryce M. Towsley photo.

footed, I suppose from the additional weight. A big buck's hooves will spread and he will step flat on his foot and on his dew claws. Older bucks with a flat-footed walk show more dew claws than a younger buck."

A buck's foot will have more rounded toes, where a doe's tend to be a lot more pointed. That may be because they travel more than does and are

heavier, both will wear them down faster. This is particularly true with mountain bucks who walk on a lot of bedrock and loose rocks. Swamp bucks will tend to have more pointed tracks.

Remember, swamps in Maine or other parts of the Northeast are not really the same as what many parts of the country think of as swamps. They are dominated by cedar, spruce, hemlock, and poplar

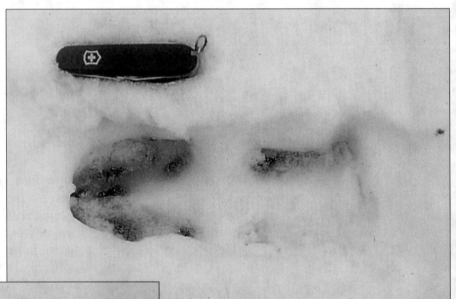

This is "Old Platterfoot," a buck that Larry hunted in 1997 but never got. The way he walks back on his feet in a flat-footed way indicates he is an old, heavy buck. Note the heavy dew claws. Bryce M. Towsley photo.

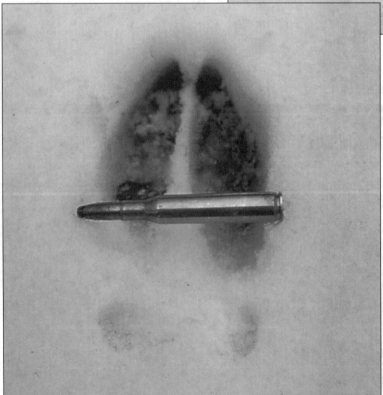

A big track from a trophy buck. Note the pointed toes indicating a "swamp" buck. Bryce M. Towsley photo.

trees. The earth will be boggy and soft, but relatively dry. There is little standing water other than in the beaver ponds or streams. The vegetation is thick, and the places along streams and beaver ponds will be choked with alders and willow. There is lots of feed, good protection from the weather, and good cover, so they can hold a lot of deer. Because gradation has filled them in over the eons, there is little bedrock, gravel, or loose rocks to wear or damage a buck's feet. While, of course, "swamp" bucks will travel up into the mountains and "mountain" bucks will venture into the swamps, each has its preferred habitat where it spends the majority of its time and its tracks will reflect that.

"Dominant bucks know they are dominant and are cocky," Larry told me. "I have seen them ap-

proach another buck and stand right up on their tip-toes as they do, taking short steps on their tiptoes as they approach each other. If you find where a buck has done that you can be sure it is a pretty good buck.

"Of course it's hard to tell a 190-pound buck from a 220-pound buck," Larry continues. "He might have weighed 240 or 250 pounds when the rut started, but they run themselves pretty thin by late in the season. You can't go by the size of his feet to judge weight, that won't change even though the weight has. Also consider that two men might have size 11 feet and one might weigh 240 pounds while the other one may go 175 pounds. It's no different with deer. You need to look at how deep he is sinking into the ground with each step to get an idea of how heavy he really is. You must consider that

This tree was rubbed by a buck Larry was tracking. Note the fresh bark on the snow. Bryce M. Towsley photo.

Wide, staggered spacing suggests that this is a big buck. His chest is wide, which the track indicates. Bryce M. Towsley photo.

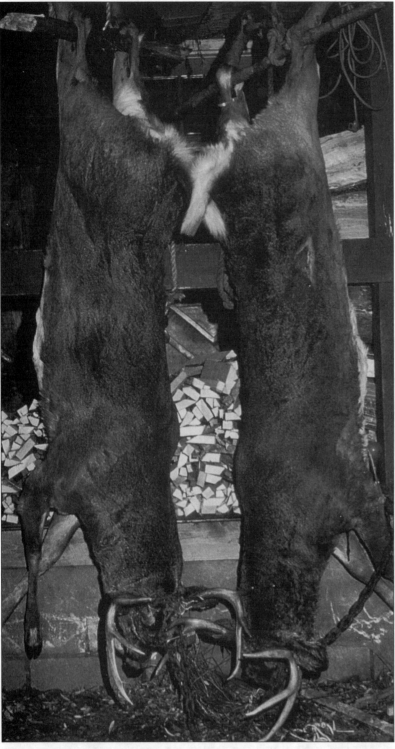

A 284-pound, 8-point taken by Lane in 1987 (left). This is the largest buck taken to date by the Benoit family. The buck on the right is 238 pounds. The chains tied to the antlers help prevent theft. Benoit photo.

ground there, how soft it is, and how much vegetation is present. Grass or leaves can support the buck and keep him from sinking deep even though he is heavy. Also the temperature is important; obviously frozen dirt will not show tracks as deep as will soft mud. Even cold, but not frozen, mud will not be as 'squishy' as mud that is in the sun absorbing warmth. It takes years of studying tracks before you really get a handle on how to do it, but a little thinking and common sense will go a long way in identifying tracks.

"The size of the foot is not as important as most hunters think. A big heavy buck can have a small foot and a small buck can have a big foot. In 1997 Lanny and Landon followed a buck that looked like he should be a big fella. When they finally caught up with him he wouldn't weigh 185 pounds, so they let him go. That buck will be a real bruiser some day after he grows up a little.

"If you follow a buck for a while and get a feel for his average stride you can start to tell how big he might be. A long deer will take a longer average stride where a shorter-bodied deer will have a shorter average stride. Of course a shorter deer will usually weigh less."

Lane says, "I like a big, heavy track of course like everybody, but I also like a big, long stride, I like a lot of distance between strides. That tells me I am after a big, rangy old buck.

He continues, "I also like indications of carrying good antlers. In addition to the other signs of a good rack I look for where sometimes the antlers will catch brush as he is walking along and will break off some of the small branches and I can get an indication of how big his rack is from that. They don't do it often, though, because they spend the summer protecting their antlers and they never really lose that tendency. I think that by spending so much time protecting their racks when they are in velvet they learn how to move through the thick woods without hanging up their horns.

Lane also says, "I am really impressed when I find a place where he encounters other bucks and runs them all off. That means he is the dominant buck. Dominance can change from day to day and he may not be the dominant buck every day, but he is that day, which is a good sign.

"If he is with a doe and lots of other bucks are around, but he is the only one that is sticking with the doe, that means he is the dominant deer in the area. If you are in a big buck area you know you have a corker on your hands."

He continues, "Of course that doesn't mean the others are not good bucks. In 1996 I was tracking a big buck when I came on one he had run off. It was late in the season (the last day!) and even later in the day. It wasn't looking like I was going to get the one I was tracking that day, so I took him. He had come in on the track and was sniffing out the doe and the dominant buck. He had a 20-inch inside spread, 22 inches outside, and 9 points. He weighed 185 pounds dressed, even though he was as thin as a rail. Earlier in the season before he had rutted off all that weight he would have gone 220 or better. He had also been beat up a lot, which gives you an idea of the size of the bucks in the area.

"There were three or four bucks like that trying to move on that doe all day long, but the big fella kept them all away. When you see where two bucks met and one chased the other away and it kept running, that usually means you are after a pretty good buck.

Shane Benoit with a 185-pound, 8-point he took in 1993. Benoit photo.

"In this situation it's hard to keep with the track of the buck you are after. With all those buck tracks running over each other it can become confusing. Instead of trying to stay with his track, keep watching the doe tracks, because he will try to stay with her. Even if he gets run off by another more dominant buck you are still ahead of the game, because that one is likely to be bigger. The biggest buck is the one that is going to be with that hot doe and he is the one you want.

"Reading tracks is not an exact science, and you can wind up shooting a buck that is not the one you are after. Sometimes you are after a good buck, you have been trailing him for a while and suddenly

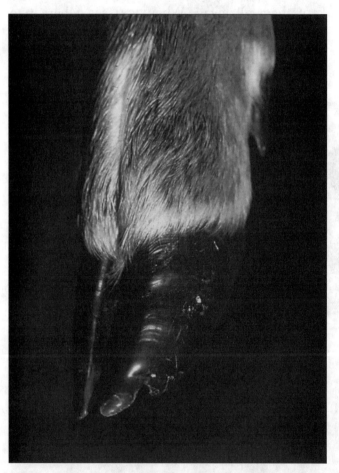

Chips such as the one in this deer's foot can make a track distinctive. They can also provide clues to where the buck spends his time. Bryce M. Towsley photo.

there is a buck standing there and it looks good. You know that if you hesitate a lot of times you lose, so you shoot. Sometimes it is a different buck than the one you have been after. He's smaller, one of the satellite bucks that are hanging around, but you put your tag on it and drag it out. It is still a buck that most people would give their eye teeth for.

"Last year I saw a deer and I kept looking it over for too long and it took off—I never saw it again. It was bare-ground and it was too tough to track him. I should have shot him, he was pretty good."

Lane agrees that track width is the key. "That buck I killed last year had a big foot and a long track, but he wasn't as wide as the one I was after, the dominant buck."

Larry points out that in a deer's track the back foot falls into the front track and the back foot covers the front one. So, you are looking at the back foot all the time. He says to look for distinctive things, chips or cracks, size, spread, the way he puts the foot down, on his toes or flat-footed. Look at the dew claws and the distance between them. Maybe they have a chip that shows once in a while or maybe one points in an odd direction. Sometimes big, heavy bucks will point their toes out when they walk, much like a fat man.

Shane and I were hunting in 1997 when we came upon several tracks. "Look at that track and tell me what is unique about the buck," he said.

"On his left foot, one side of his hoof is shorter than the other," I replied with an arrogant smirk.

"What about that track," Shane asked?

"Same deer."

"Look again and this time pay attention."

I finally realized that while this deer also had one side of his foot shorter, it was the other side. There were two bucks. Paying attention is important.

Larry once hunted a big buck with a hoof that crossed over itself from an injury. He saw the buck's tracks a lot and followed him every time he had a chance. The buck would make the same big swing about every two days, ending by going into a big swamp to bed. There wasn't much snow, and in the swamp there was hardly any, so he kept losing the track once he entered the swamp. Even after the snow came the buck would always go into the swamp in the afternoons when it was too late to follow. He never got that buck.

Another buck had a hoof that had been broken in the joint. Apparently he had stepped on a rock or root and his weight had caused the hoof to separate. He weighed 230 dressed and probably 275 pounds or more live weight. With all of the weight on one side, he had split his hoof. The foot developed a large growth as it tried to heal, and he was easy to follow. That one didn't get away, and Larry boiled the foot out to save as a keepsake of a great hunt.

You can tell a lot about where a buck spends his time by his track. Old mountain deer that live in rocky terrain have more rounded tracks. The rocks and rough terrain wear the sharp edges off more quickly. A buck that lives in the swamps will be walking on softer ground and his tracks will be more pointed, with sharper edges. If a buck is traveling in search of does and you know the area well, you can use this information to figure out where he might be spending his days bedded down, and it can save you hours of tracking. A buck is going to return to a familiar place, a place he feels safe. If it is a mountain buck, look for his tracks in the spruce high up near the top. A swamp buck will, of course, head for the swampy lowland bogs.

Aging a track is a lot tougher. Of course, if it is snowing you can tell quickly how old it is by the amount of snow in the track. If there is not a lot of snow you know that the buck is pretty close to you. The problem is that 15 minutes later the track might look old when it really is not.

Shane cites an example of exactly that. "I found a track a few years ago and could barely make it out. It was snowing pretty hard and I knew that it probably wasn't all that old. I followed it, and that buck had my tag on him in a short while."

One trick is to step beside the track and compare how your track looks next to the deer's. Watch how the snow crumbles and how it is crumbled in the deer's track. Try to compare that

to the temperature in recent hours. Remember that a track made in the late afternoon might be in snow that was soft and slightly melting, where by morning the temperature has dropped and the snow is frozen and crumbly.

Check the edges of the track to see if they are sharp and crisp. The longer a track has been around the less sharp it is, because the weather breaks it down. Even on a cold day the sun can melt the edges of a track and age it, in mud or snow. Temperature plays a big part in how fast a track ages. So does moisture—wet snow will melt for several reasons. Just the act of a deer stepping in the snow will create heat, and if the temperature is borderline it can continue to melt at a rate that will

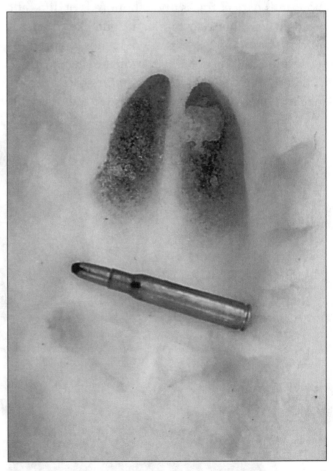

This track is as wide as a .30-06 shell. This is a good buck, likely to weigh more than 200 pounds. Bryce M. Towsley photo.

make a track look older than it really is. If the ground is wet and snow is over it, there will be a lot of moisture disturbed by the deer stepping on the ground. This can melt and age the track and fool you into thinking it is older than it is. But, if you find a track that is still slowly filling with water or one that is muddy when the water around is not, get on it—that buck is close.

The key is to study the track and use your brain. Think about when that deer might have made the track and what the temperature and weather were doing then and for the last couple of days. Does what you expect to see fit with what you are seeing? If not, what does? Maybe that track is older or fresher than you think it is. Aging a track is likely the most difficult part of tracking deer. It truly requires that you look at thousands of deer tracks under hundreds of different weather conditions to master it, but like Shane is quick to point out, "It is really a matter of common sense and thinking about what you are seeing."

Like Larry says, "A lot of hunters can't recognize a track from a specific buck and they may be on two or three bucks in the course of a day and not even know it."

Good trackers will try to identify individual deer by their tracks. They will see a buck's track one time and recognize it when they see it again, even if it is miles away and days later. To do this, learn to watch for the little things that make it different from the other deer tracks in the area.

"One time I was on a big buck when I crossed his track again," Larry said. "I knew that he had made a big loop and was headed back up on the mountain. By recognizing his track I saved myself miles and miles of tracking. It seemed like every deer in the woods was on the move that day, and there were lots and lots of tracks. But I had studied his track until I could recognize it."

"I killed that buck too," he told me.

"I used a piece of wood that I cut off to measure the width of his track and it helped to recognize him later. I kept that stick for a souvenir for years after that."

Bucks from 1994. Benoit photo.

Chapter 5

On the Trail

"After a few weeks of this a transformation happens, suddenly you feel like a new man. You have a new outlook on everything, you are alive. You feel like lifting your head up and howling like a wolf. Your arms feel like steel and your legs are so strong, you feel like you can walk 20 miles without getting worn out. My friend, when you begin to feel like this, you are becoming a deer hunter!

-Larry Benoit

Years back, when I was in my free-wheeling "bachelor phase," I shared an apartment with a couple of other footloose rubes. Dominating the living room of that hovel was the mounted head of a massive whitetail.

While I doubt it would make the minimum for a Boone & Crockett book entry, it was deer enough to be considered a trophy in the mind of even the most jaded of whitetail hunters. It had 10 long, evenly matched points in its wide, heavy, and very symmetrical rack. To me, a rabid whitetail hunter, it was a work of art, a true thing of beauty. It had but one inherent flaw—it wasn't mine.

The roommate who had shot it was no more a deer hunter than I was a preacher. If there was a mistake to make in whitetail hunting, he had made it. He had no real passion or drive to be a deer hunter, but was there simply because that's what his friends were doing and he didn't want to be left behind. The head on the wall meant not that he was a good deer hunter, but only that he had been in the right place, at the right time, one time!

This only reinforced the old adage that anyone can get lucky and kill a big deer. The fact that he had never taken another buck before or after that one confirmed it.

It is well accepted that hunters who kill big bucks with any degree of regularity do not rely (as he did) entirely on luck. They work hard, hone their skills, and are relentless when the season is open. If there is one thing that marks the hunter who will take trophy bucks with any regularity it is a solid drive to succeed. The hunter who is consistent in taking 200-pound plus bucks year after year will have a single-minded determination that borders on the obsessive.

It's like Larry says, "Tracking big bucks is a lot like boxing. Often the results depend on how badly you want it. The man who wants to win the most, the man who keeps going no matter what is usually the one who succeeds. Tracking deer is much the same.

"If you stay with one particular buck and make up your mind he is the one you want, you can get him. I have stayed as long as fourteen days on a buck. The Vermont season was only sixteen days long, but I got him the next to the last day of the season.

"You have to keep at it day after day, no matter what. Just because you are tired from the day before, you can't give up. If it's storming or cold outside you have to go anyway. Like I said, it's like boxing. Just because you get knocked down in the first round are you going to quit? Not if you want to win. Get up and come back, use your knowledge, use the mistakes to learn, make them stepping stones. If you make the same mistakes every time you go deer hunting you aren't going to accomplish a thing. You need to learn, to grow, to progress as a hunter. If you couple that with a drive to keep going no matter what, you can become a trophy buck hunter.

"You will never fulfill your dream of a big buck until you get out and try. Get out and go to the places other hunters won't go. Get to the big woods and work at it, study the ways of the whitetail.

"Somewhere out there at the end of those tracks is your dream buck. The sweat is running down your face, your feet are telling you they can go no more. You have a cramp between your shoulder blades from carrying your rifle and you feel like you are drained. At the end of the day you realize that you have 8 or 10 miles to get out of the woods, and then you look down at those big tracks and think to yourself what you would have done if you had shot him back there, how on earth would you ever get him out? You know, though, that the next day you will go back and get on him again. He is going to lay down sometime and you will want to be there when he does.

"You get back to camp, drag your boots off, fall out of your hunting pants, climb into bed, and dream of your big buck. At 3:30 or 4:00, you awake and fall out of bed stiff and lame. You get into your pants, still wet from the day before, and limp off to get some food into your belly, and then you go back into the woods and pick up the tracks again.

"After a few weeks of this a transformation happens, suddenly you feel like a new man. You have a new outlook on everything, you are alive. You feel like lifting your head up and howling like a wolf. Your arms feel like steel and your legs are so strong, you feel like you can walk 20 miles without

getting worn out. My friend, when you begin to feel like this, you are becoming a deer hunter!

"Your wildest dream can happen today. The track that you are on begins to look better, your eyes are sharper, you can smell the woods, it's coming together now. Somewhere up ahead of you he is there, you have been reading the signs that he has left behind. He is getting careless now, from time to time he is slowing down to browse. He is smelling the woods looking for a doe in heat. You are just as cool as a card shark playing his hand. He is in front of you, your hard work has paid off, all that pain you had when you woke up this morning means nothing. Your nose is running, but you don't make a sound, you don't dare sniff. Your rifle comes up and the safety is slipped off. You line up the red bead on his rib cage. Your finger is on the trigger.

"There will be many songs around the old stove as the nights go by and you tell your story over and

Larry in 1954. The buck on the left was taken by daughter Lona, the center deer was taken by Lanny, and Larry took the buck on the right. Benoit photo.

over. As you relive the chase of trailing the big swamp buck, you will forget how hard it was to get him out of the woods."

Is there any doubt that Larry has lived all of this?

The rut plays an important role in most tracking. Of course you can hunt successfully during other times of the season, but the rut has the big bucks not only moving, but preoccupied and primed to make a mistake. A big, dominant buck has only one thing on his mind during this time: finding does in heat and breeding them. He will travel endlessly in search of receptive does, which has him leaving more tracks in more places than he normally would. His single-mindedness will have him traveling more or less in a straight line from doe to doe. He may spend some time with a doe in estrus, but when she is done, he's gone.

During this time, the buck will eat very little and will bed only when he is worn out, and then likely for only a few hours at a time. This constant move-

ment, coupled with the distraction of breeding, makes him easier to kill than at any other time of the year—not easy...but easier!

One of the things you look to do when tracking a deer is to catch him up and walking away from you. He will usually be traveling into or across the wind, trying to snatch a whiff of a doe in heat. When you catch him in these circumstances, he is vulnerable. You are behind him where he is not usually watching, and the wind is in your favor. He is distracted by the rut, and you have a good chance of killing him the first time you catch up to him.

The next best thing is to catch him in his bed. When he is bedded he will not be moving, and so every step you take is another step closer to him. The downside is that he will be alert to danger. You must read the sign and know when he is bedded or about to bed. Then you must react accordingly.

A lot of times a buck will bed where he can watch his back track. If you keep blundering

Larry on a buck's track in 1997. Bryce M. Towsley photo.

along on the track, all you will see is a blur as he disappears. You must read the sign and know when to slow down into what the Benoits call the "death creep."

The secret is in knowing when to slow down and when it's time to cover ground. Many hunters creep along the track the entire time they are hunting, trying to be quiet and moving slow. They have their guns up and are ready to shoot at any time. Their nerves are taut, and not only will this burn them out quickly, but they will likely never catch the buck this way. You have to know when it is time to sling the rifle and cover some ground and when it is time to get your gun in your hand, slow down, and be ready. That is the art of reading the track and it is the key to success.

If a buck is all alone and traveling on a course that is straight, and it is obvious that he is doing nothing but moving, covering ground, and looking for does, your only hope is to lay down some tracks yourself. That is assuming that the track is relatively fresh. If the buck has a 10-hour head start on you and keeps covering ground at that rate you simply can't catch him. However, if you think that the track is very fresh or that the buck may be headed into where some does are hanging out or a place where he may decide to bed, then it is a track worth following. Sling your gun and make tracks yourself. Walk at a fast pace, but watch the sign. That buck can decide at any time to bed down.

Part of knowing when he is going to bed is knowing the habits of whitetail deer. If the track was made in the last darkness of approaching morning and it is headed to a thick spruce knob on top of a mountain, then it is a good bet that the buck is on his way to lie down. This is a good track to fol-

Shane checks out where a buck nipped some browse. Sometimes a buck will feed as he walks, giving little indication that he is going to bed. A sharp hunter will notice the sign and be prepared; one less observant will likely bump the buck from his bed. Bryce M. Towsley photo.

low, and if you do things right, you have a good chance of seeing this buck, but only if you read the sign and slow down when you are close to his bed.

If the track is simply headed out across miles and miles of hardwood ridges, then he is probably looking for does and it may be hard to catch up with him. If you are to have a chance at all you must move fast. If memory serves me right, it was Bill Jordan (the writer, trick shooter, and border patrolman, not the camo guy) who said about gunfighting, "Take your time, FAST!." The same might apply to tracking a deer.

The biggest single reason that most hunters fail to see the deer they are tracking is that they do not move fast enough. The buck may have several hour's start on you, and he is traveling on four legs instead of two. If you pussyfoot around you will never catch up. Hunters need to be able to cover ground fast to catch up to the deer, while at the same time they need to be as quiet as possible and alert so that they see the buck before the buck sees them. They must also read the sign to know when it is time to slow down and pussyfoot along.

Boiled down, it is the art of tracking and many never master it.

If the track is headed into a deep swamp it is anybody's guess what that buck has on his mind. He may be ready to bed, or he may be just passing though looking for does. You can only tell by following it until you see.

The best sign that a buck is getting ready to bed is that he will almost always eat a little first. If the deer is meandering and munching here and there on buds or pawing the ground for ferns or beechnuts, he may be getting ready to bed for a while. Inexperienced trackers may not realize this and keep charging ahead; you can be sure that they will spook the buck. However, woods-wise hunters recognize the sign and slow down. They hunt carefully and slowly now, picking the woods apart with their eyes. They move only after seeing everything within their range of vision. Soon, maybe they will see the deer and the game is over.

Look for his track to slow down and to meander a little as he feeds. Watch for nipped browse, which is the most common feed in early winter in the north country. But also notice if he is eating ferns or beechnuts that he has pawed up. Watch for where he has placed his mouth to the ground to pick up something to eat. Sometimes this is easy to miss if the buck simply grabbed something off the ground. It may not be as obvious as stopping to paw the ground, but it might be only a slight indentation in the snow from his nose.

Any time you see a buck feeding it is a good sign that he is getting ready to bed, which means that it is time to slow down, be quiet, be ready, and pay attention. Sometimes, though, a buck will simply grab a nip of browse here and there as he walks along. His tracks may not indicate a lot of difference, and to notice it you will usually have to watch the brush along his path. A less than observant tracker may miss this, because the nipped branches are not all that obvious. He may not even break stride as he feeds, but still he is bedded down just ahead. If you miss the sign and keep walking quickly you will jump him out of his bed, usually without a shot.

You must learn to recognize not only that he is feeding, but also that he is approaching a place to bed. This is not always a mountain top or a deep swamp. Bucks will often bed on hardwood benches along the mountain side where they can watch their back trail. They also like grown clear-cuts, often bedding beside brush piles or on hills where they can watch their back tracks. They will usually circle to one side or the other before they bed. It is important to watch all around you, looking to both sides. If you see that the track suddenly turns and hooks right or left, be extra careful—he is real close.

"I have shot a lot of bucks in their beds," says Lanny. "Most never knew I was there." When you start to do the same you know you are becoming a deer tracker.

If the tracks indicate that the buck is traveling with a doe that may be in heat anything is possible. Not only is he trying to breed the doe, but he will also be constantly running off other suitors. While all of this will delay him and make him easier to catch, it also adds more eyes and ears to the game as well as a level of unpredictability. You may be on a track that is moving along and thinking that he is far ahead when suddenly he is there in front of you chasing off another buck. The key here is to stay focused and ready, but to try your best to interpret the sign so you don't get left behind. Sure, you will make mistakes and even spook deer when you couldn't have done anything different, but, keep after him. He won't run far and he will be a lot more interested in that doe than he is in you, so stay with the track no matter what.

If there are several bucks after the same doe and the tracks become hard to follow, look for the doe's tracks. They will be obviously different from the bucks' and likely easier to follow. The bucks will go where she goes, and you can be assured that the largest, most dominant buck is the one that will be sticking closest to her. Keep watching too for the "satellite" bucks that are being kept away by the dominant buck. They can still be big, trophy bucks. They are frustrated, mad, and primed to make a mistake. It isn't unheard of for one to mistake your footsteps for those of another deer and come over to check you out.

Shane points out that one reason some hunters track a deer all day without seeing him is because they aren't looking for him properly. It is not only a lack of concentration but also a lack of not reading the sign. Watching the track too much is a common mistake with a lot of hunters. They walk along with their heads down, watching only the track, and they miss the deer. You must watch all around you while still watching the track. Of course you must see the track, but don't become so focused that you miss what is happening around you. Watch the track with your peripheral vision, looking directly at it only when you need to sort out a problem. When you are in a tough situation and you have to look at the track to sort it out, make sure that you look up and all around at regular intervals. Never stare at the track for more than a few

seconds at a time; keep your eyes moving. Shift your vision out to the furthest you can see and make sure you look at all of the land in between. It is easy to be looking off in the distance and miss a deer right in front of you. It doesn't even have to be a long distance; in many places you may only be able to see less than 100 yards, but in concentrating to see into the brush at that distance you may overlook a buck bedded 25 yards in front of you. You must be aware of all that is in your field of vision, including, of course, the tracks.

Another thing that makes the big trophy buck vulnerable to the tracker is the buck's experience, and this is where the determination of the hunter comes into play. The buck that has been around long enough to become a trophy has dealt with humans before. There simply isn't enough truly remote land in the whitetail's domain for a deer to survive four or five hunting seasons without having some experience with humans. Any buck worth hunting likely knows how the game is played. He's had hunters on his trail before and knows that after 3 or 4 miles they are going to give up. The smart buck knows how to react. He doesn't work any harder than he has to and he stays just ahead and out of sight. Then along comes a tracker with some determination, who stays on the track. When he is still there after 3 or 4 miles, the buck gets a little worried. After 6 or 7 miles he is like Butch and Sundance asking, "Who is this guy?" A few more miles and he is getting used to your presence; he has been living with you on his backside, and though you may have jumped him several times, as far as he is concerned nothing has happened, so maybe you are more an annoyance than a threat. It is likely that he will become frustrated and curious. He wants to know who you are and why you are staying after him. You may start to notice places where he stopped and looked back at you, trying to see just what you are. He may even get a little angry at you, and anger clouds his judgment. Stay focused, because he is making mistakes. Sooner or later he will linger too long trying to get a look, and you need to be constantly alert because

one of these times he will show himself. If you are ready, he's yours.

Of course, like people, every deer is different and each will react differently. That's where a woodsman earns his keep. An experienced tracker can read the deer and predict how he will react. The key is in reading the track, knowing the land, and predicting correctly what the buck will do. The only true way to learn to do these things is by experience, by following a lot of deer tracks. Get out

A buck that Shane and Bryce were tracking rubbed this tree after getting up from his bed. Note the bark on top of the snow. In spite of it being early afternoon and a sunny day, the chips have not melted into the snow or blown away. This indicates that the buck may be close. Bryce M. Towsley photo.

there and track bucks even when it isn't hunting season. Follow them and learn how a mature buck thinks. Learn what he will likely do in a given situation. Of course there will be surprises, for deer are full of them, but they are not that complicated—their brains are a lot less developed than a human's. No matter how smart a buck is, most people are a lot smarter. It is just that they think differently than humans, and you need to learn that. We need to adopt the way a deer thinks and not the way we think that they should think.

A buck in rut may rub trees and make scrapes as he travels along. When you encounter a fresh rub, look at the shavings on the ground and think about what is happening. Is the sun out today? If it is, even when the temperature is below freezing the darker bark and shavings will absorb the sun's heat and melt down into the snow. Have they done that? If so, how far? If they have sunk into the snow a good bit it is likely that buck is still far ahead of you, but if they are resting on top of the snow as if they just fell there, perhaps he is close. Of course that depends on the sun and the time of day. You must consider how long it has been shining, because the effect will be a lot more pronounced in the afternoon than the morning. If the sun is not out the chips may rest on top all day long, particularly if it stays cold, so watch for other signs. Is the wind blowing? Are the shavings blown all around yet? The scraped portion of a tree will age quickly as it dries. Take your knife and, using the back of the blade, scrape a new place beside where he has rubbed. Then look at how it compares to the part that the buck rubbed. Are they nearly the same? If so, he may be close.

If you find a scrape he has made, check to see how fresh it looks. Often the ground has not yet frozen under the snow and the dirt is still relatively soft. See if it has frozen after losing the insulating qualities from the snow. Kick the snow off another patch of dirt close to the scrape and compare the two. Has the dirt in the scrape started to dry at all or is it still moist even on the edges? The best place to judge this is in the tracks he has left in the scrape and where he has dragged his hooves. The sharp ridges he has pawed up or on the tracks themselves will be the first to dry out and deteriorate. Has the wind blown snow or debris into the scrape? If it is snowing, how much has accumulated in the scrape? Look at the overhanging branch and see how fresh the wood looks where he has rubbed off the bark or broken the branches.

This is a good time, too, to judge how big this buck is. How high did he reach to work the overhanging branch? Remember that he will rub his eye on the branch as well as reach up to break branches with his antlers. This can help you judge his size and the height of his antlers, by comparing the distance between the two. Get down and smell the scrape. If it is fresh you will smell his urine very strongly. Remember, too, that he is likely working this scrape because he expects other deer to be close by. He may be slowing down to work more scrapes or he may have found some does, so slow down a little and watch carefully.

A rutting old buck is a raunchy fellow and his bed will retain a musty, musky smell for a while after he leaves. If you get down and smell it you can gain more knowledge on how far ahead he is. Look at the tracks leaving the bed. Are they running or simply walking off? If they are walking you likely didn't spook him out of the bed; he left on his own. If they are running you may have spooked him, which is good and bad—good because you are close, bad because he knows you are after him.

When you jump a buck and he runs off, sling your rifle and start laying tracks as fast as you can keep up the pace. But, watch the sign. It's like Larry says, "Usually they won't run a mile, so you need to be watching the sign for when he slows down. If he is tired and wants to lie down he may run a little and then find another bed. You need to watch the track to see what he is doing. But, sometimes they will run all day. If you have one that runs like that you probably won't get him. It's better to find another buck. But if you simply must have that one, you have to stay with him day after day until he gets tired of running. Then, if he is a wise old buck, he will start running again. It won't be easy."

Shane says, "The deer may know you are after him when you jump him up, but he doesn't think like you and me. He isn't thinking all the time that somebody is after him. Deer get spooked all the time and it's rare that whatever spooks them will keep following the trail. After a while he will forget or assume that you are no longer on his trail. Lots of times a buck that I have jumped doesn't know I am behind him—until it's too late."

Larry says, "Any buck that knows you are after him will be always looking back at you and you have to read the sign to know. Lots of times they

Shane checks out the bed of a buck. Note the stain from the hocks on the rear leg. This helps to confirm that it is a buck. The size of the bed indicates a mature trophy buck. Bryce M. Towsley photo.

are looking back when you shoot them. They get careless, they don't necessarily think like a human and they don't realize that you have a rifle that makes you dangerous for a longer distance than the predators they are used to dealing with."

Lane points out another common problem encountered on a smart buck's trail: trying to sort out a big track in a swamp full of deer tracks.

"When he has been over the swamp you can spend all day trying to sort it all out. I look for exit points and start following them. Sometimes they turn right back into the swamp and you might as well start looking for another exit point because you are going right back into that same mess. Sooner or later you will find where he left for good. Or

if you don't and you have circled the swamp, you know he is still in there and you can go in after him. Then you have to work real slow because he is in there and likely close.

"A lot of guys will spend all day trying to sort the track out and they run out of time. That buck may have found all the does, checked to see if they were ready to breed, and found out what he wanted to know and he is gone. If he hasn't left, that's the time to work in there slow.

"Lots of hunters get so exasperated with trying to figure it all out that they get sloppy and start to walk fast and look too much at the track. They lose caution. That's when the buck is standing there

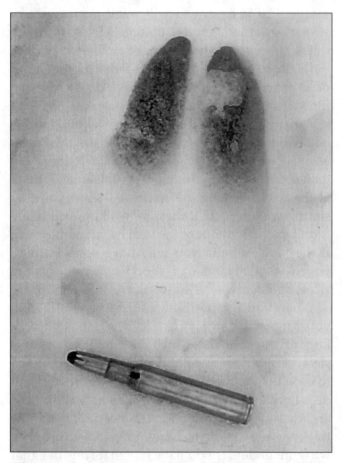

This track belongs to a good buck, which likely weighs more than 200 pounds. The track is as wide as a .30-06 shell. Note the slight difference in the toes and that the left is more pointed than the right. Remembering this will help you identify any tracks as being made by this buck. Bryce M. Towsley photo.

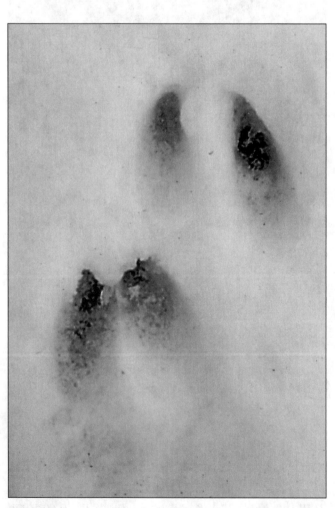

This buck stopped and stood here for a moment, during which he placed his foot down twice. Bryce M. Towsley photo.

watching them, and then he is gone out of there. If they had just kept their head up and kept looking instead of watching the ground they could have taken their buck.

"You are going to run into this situation almost every time you track a buck, and if you can't deal with it you will never be successful as a tracker."

Larry points out that, "A lot of times the guys will see the track leaving, and because they don't recognize it they think it's a different track so they go back into the swamp to look for him. Pretty soon it's time to leave and you have wasted the whole day. You must be able to recognize the track of the buck you are after.

"A lot of hunters can't recognize a track as belonging to a certain deer and they may be on two or three bucks in the course of a day and not even

know it. You can waste a lot of time this way and never catch up to any of them."

At every seminar the Benoits give, somebody will ask, "What kind of scent do you use."

"Common sense," is the standard reply.

But, that isn't entirely true. Shane showed me a secret while we were on a track. Every time we came to a place where a deer had urinated he would take some of the urine soaked snow and rub it on his wool pants.

"By the end of the season they smell pretty bad," Shane said. "But, it can give me the little extra edge in confusing the buck just enough to gain a split second. Sometimes that's enough.

"I prefer to use urine I find in the woods because it is natural and is what that deer smells every day. It is from deer that buck knows, and they are eating

Quite a line up of bucks from 1996. Benoit photo.

plants that he is familiar with. I think that what they eat affects how the urine smells. Just like ours smells different when we have been drinking coffee. Only with a deer it is more subtle. With a commercial scent it is something he is not used to. They may work fine, but I know this is better.

"Sometimes, too, we will rub cedar on our clothes to help mask our scent. It won't cover the smell of a man completely, nothing will, but it can't hurt and it smells better than urine."

If the snow is old and crusty, or if it is very cold, it will be noisy walking. This makes your task a little tougher. However, the deer will usually know that you are behind him long before you shoot anyway, so while noisy walking certainly doesn't make things any easier, it doesn't necessarily make tracking up a buck impossible. One thing to keep in mind is that when the deer is close, and it is cat and mouse time, you need to be extra aware of the noise the walking is making. Walk on rocks, logs, or anything you can to keep the noise down, and keep hoping that the weather will change and bring you better conditions.

We make do with the days the good Lord and vacation schedules give us to hunt, but if we could custom order one, the day would have about 5 inches of fresh snow. The temperature would be just above the freezing point, making the snow a soft, slightly wet cushion under our feet (in addition to muffling sounds, this soft snow shows a track very well). The trees and bushes would be bent under the new snow, and on the very best days a soft, big-flaked snow would continue to fall.

Some 1980 bucks from Maine. Benoit photo.

This is a killing day, and if you find a big track early in the morning, that deer should be yours before dark. Move fast and silently on the track and you may just kill the buck the first time you catch up to him.

Hemingway wrote about weather such as this and how it makes the animals easy to approach. He was right. They seem a little less wary on this kind of day. Perhaps the falling snow and the changed landscape confuse the deer. Who knows, but it's a day to track and that's what the smart hunter is doing.

The Benoits rarely advised leaving the track. "You just never know where the buck is going. You may lose the track or you might run into the deer and bump him, it's just plain risky." This sentiment is almost universal among hard-core trackers, however, other hunters have had success with modification to the party line. Sometimes bucks will circle back to where you started, particularly if they are limited in the territory. In Maine where the country is big they are likely to just light out and cover a lot of ground. Like Lane says, "They get headed like they have a compass and they don't stop." But, in places with smaller blocks of woods, such as in Vermont, they have a tendency to circle. If you can recognize this you can use it to your advantage.

A friend of mine was on the trail of a big buck in the Moosehead Lake region of Maine in 1982 when he realized that on two days in a row the buck had crossed a logging road at the exact same location and at almost the same time. He had his buddy take up the trail and he went to wait at the crossing. The buck dressed out at 253 pounds!

My uncle, Errol "Butch" Towsley, used similar tactics to take a big buck in New York's Adirondacks in '85. He was trailing the buck, but the snow was old and spotty in places. As the track led into an area in which he had found many scrapes the previous day, he knew the buck would be slowing down. He became concerned about spooking the buck because of the noisy conditions, so he left the track and made a big swing, approaching slowly from the downwind side. He caught the buck at a scrape and took it with a long shot through the hardwoods. It weighed 191 pounds and carried a wide 10-point rack.

The moral of the story is that sometimes you need to improvise and break the rules. Why not? The deer do it all the time!

One important facet of tracking is knowing when to quit. There is a tendency for us all to want to stay with the track "just a little bit longer." We think that another 15 minutes can make a difference, but this is dangerous thinking. As Larry puts it, "Night falls so fast in Maine you can hear it when it hits the ground." Tracking trophy whitetail deer often involves wild and remote country, coupled with nasty late-fall weather. This is a recipe for trouble, so know when it is time to call it a day.

"In Maine we start thinking about getting out of the woods by 2:30" says Lane. "It's pretty dark in those woods by 4:30 and you don't want to spend the night. Of course, it depends on where you are. If I know I am close to a road I'll stay longer, but if I am not sure I'll head out.

"It is easier to see in the dark in hardwoods, and in Vermont where there are lots of hardwoods, I may stay a little longer. In Maine there are many more swamps and spruce. Those spruce are dangerous in the dark, you can't see well and with them being so thick it is easy to stick a stub in your eye. Also, with it being darker amongst them, it is easy to step in a hole and break a leg. This will make for a lot of trouble as we are often dressed lightly and soaked with sweat. It wouldn't take long for hypothermia to set in. Tomorrow is another day.

"If you want to track that buck the next day, start where you left off. If you chased him all day it's likely that he is tired and may wander around or bed. You may catch him in 3 or 4 hours if you are lucky. It depends on how far in I left the track and how far ahead of me I think he was. If it takes me 3 hours to get back to him it might not be worth it. Unless he is pretty good I often just go to look for another track."

Often the Benoits come out on a road that is miles from where they started, and Larry says that when he hits the road he will leave a sign for Shane

or whoever he is hunting with, then he starts walking. Whoever gets back to the rig first will start driving the roads looking for the others. As he cruises the logging roads the driver looks for boot tracks on the side of the road. Usually they will recognize the boot print, but often they may make a set of tracks and then put a stick in it to indicate that they are on the road and need a ride. It is impossible for a stick to be standing up in a track that was simply left by a walking hunter, and so the sign is positive that somebody up ahead needs a ride. They may also make an arrow on the ground to indicate the direction they are walking, particularly if it is bare-ground or the snow is gone from the road.

It is not uncommon for the driver to follow for 4 or 5 miles to catch up. That's a lot of walking, but it's all part of being a deer tracker. That, and faith and trust that your partner, will be there sooner or later.

When your deer is down and you are sitting quietly with it, experiencing the let-down that comes when it is finally over, you are certain to reflect on tracking and its difficulties. You remember the ordeal that brought you to this point, and you will think of the long drag out you are faced with and you will wonder if it is worth it.

Then you look at what is most likely the biggest buck of your life and you know the answer.

There can be only one.

Chapter 6

The End Game

"You can screw up all day long, but if you screw up in that last 200 yards, kiss it good-bye—you have wasted the day."

-Shane Benoit

When campfire talk turns to the "Benoit" style of hunting, most hunters emphasize tracking. They talk about the endurance needed to trail a buck through rough country and of the tricks that a buck can show you in his attempt to throw you off the trail. They discuss the fine points of finding and identifying a buck track

Shane Benoit. Don't watch the track so much that you miss seeing the buck. Always watch in all directions when you are on the trail. Bryce M. Towsley photo.

and they even will haughtily discuss the difficulty of pulling him out of the back country.

While all of this is infinitely important to the process, it is neither the essence of what the Benoits do, nor the most important aspect of the hunt. What separates the Benoits from the huddled masses of "wanna-be" deer trackers is their ability to play the end game successfully.

All of your efforts are directed to getting close enough to a trophy buck to be able to shoot him, yet that is exactly when most hunters blow it.

Larry confirms that when he says, "We get a lot of letters from deer hunters and a good share of them are like that, from guys who blow it at the end."

Shane points out that, "Time and time again I have had hunters tell about tracking a deer all day long and never seeing him. They say, 'I tracked him all day and kept jumping him up and jumping him up, but never saw him.' That's because they are not looking for him properly. It's a lack of concentration and also a lack of reading the sign. Tracking a buck is easy compared to finally getting close enough to shoot him."

You must train to the woods. It is not something that you can simply will yourself to do. With the demands of home, job, and life we spend 50 weeks a year in our human environment, all the while the buck is living in the woods. We cannot simply step out of our environment and into his, expecting that we will be able to kill him with ease. Have you ever seen a deer that wandered into a city? The deer is completely out of his element, totally confused, and inept at survival. Often it ends badly for the deer. We are not unlike that when we enter the deer's domain. Perhaps it is human arrogance or simply that we don't see it, but we rarely recognize or admit that we are not tuned to the woods. There is no way we can be, because it takes time to train your eyes, body, and mind to deer hunting.

Simply walking quietly in the woods is a conditioned skill. It takes a few days to shift from our normal walking patterns; you must change the cadence and pace of your steps. You must also change the way you place your feet on the ground. You must become an animal yourself and blend with the woods. (Larry stressed this again and again.) Slow down, and be aware of what's on the ground and how you will use it to your advantage. Shane once killed a very large buck under extremely noisy bare-ground conditions by walking on stones and logs to keep the noise to a minimum.

Lanny adds a tip: on packy snow that is noisy as you step, slide your foot in under the snow to make less noise. This is simply another illustration of experience being the best teacher. You must walk on a variety of ground conditions to learn how to react to each one.

Learn to roll your weight onto your foot and to "feel" what is underneath. Never allow yourself to be off balance so much that you can't react to a stick that is about to break. You must be able to instantly remove your weight from that foot and to pick it up and place it in another location. That means that you will need to not only slow down from your careless "city" walking style, but that you must also shorten your steps. By taking shorter steps you maintain your center of balance be-

Shane Benoit shooting at a running buck. Sometimes a change in perspective, such as squatting down, will open a lane that allows you to see further into the brush. Bryce M. Towsley photo.

tween both feet so that you can instantly shift your weight to either leg.

Learn to "snake" your way though the woods so that you can avoid branches by simply twisting your body a little. The trick is to keep the movement to a minimum and make it flow smoothly. Movement will always tip off a buck to your presence, but rapid or jerky movement will alert him sooner. Learn how to weave your body through the brush in a fluid motion and without moving your hands. Hand movement is a giveaway to a buck, particularly if you are not wearing gloves to hide the unnatural color of your skin. If you do wear gloves, make sure they are not a bright color.

The only things you should be moving when a buck is close are your eyes and head. Moving the head is a necessary compromise to spotting a buck, however, it should be a slow, smooth, and methodical movement. As Larry puts it, "You need to wear out your shirt collar as you move your head back and forth. That deer can be anyplace and you have to keep looking. The movement of your head is necessary to see in all places at all times. It is worse in a swamp than on a mountain top because a buck can be anyplace in a swamp, where on a mountain top it is more directional. You are peeking over ridges and in terrain that is more broken and there are fewer places for the buck to bed. That's why I prefer hunting mountain bucks.

"Don't look for movement, it's too late then. The first movement you will likely see is a switch of his tail and less than two seconds after he moves his tail, he's gone. When you are close to a buck you must be ready. Keep your gun up and your finger on the safety ready to push it off and shoot at all

This buck is lying where he fell after Larry shot him. Also shown is Larry's rifle. Benoit photo.

times. Look over the sights for the deer and keep the gun pointed where you are looking.

"Don't ever cough, and if you have to sneeze, choke it off. [He notes that after eating camp food for a week this may mean you will have to change your pants later.] Don't sniff, spit, or make any noise. If your nose is running, let it run. The buck will usually know you are out there, but you must keep him off balance about exactly where."

Larry illustrates this well, "I was guiding a fella one time who was a heavy smoker. All morning I kept hearing the 'clink' of his Zippo lighter as he lit yet another cigarette. I asked him time and again not to smoke, but he paid no attention. 'A deer can't hear that,' he kept saying. Finally we were close, real close, and I knew that we would see this buck very soon. Then behind me I heard 'clink.' The buck blew up out of his bed right in front of us and was gone. I took that fool back to camp. We were never going to kill a buck as long as he refused to listen to me."

Larry further instructs, "Keep the gun up because he will see the motion when you raise it if you have it down by your side. If you have time, slide the safety off slowly to keep noise down. We get lots of letters and comments about the Remington pump rifles rattling. Sure they will rattle if you grab one and shake it, but these rifles do not rattle in the woods. Part of this is because the forend is in your hand as you close in on a buck. Look at that wall over there [he was pointing to a wall in his living room that is completely covered with deer antlers] and tell me if you think that we did that with rifles that rattle and scare deer?

"Back in 1995 I had a big 250-pound buck that was looking right at me when I saw him. My rifle was on him just as soon as I spotted him and I just watched. I couldn't see the other side of his antlers, so I waited until he turned his head and I saw those big antlers. Just then his tail wiggled which meant he was about to go, but it was too late—'boom!' Most hunters would have had the gun down and would not have gotten the shot off. I knew he was going to be there someplace as I came up over the top of the ridge, so I was ready. I didn't have the gun down by my side and I wasn't scratching my nose. I had the gun up and I was ready. I was on full alert. If I hadn't been I would not have killed that buck."

Larry very rarely shoots twice. "Make sure the first one is good and you don't have to," he points out.

Shane looks at a tree that has been rubbed by so many bucks over a period of years that it died (because of extensive bark damage). He is looking at nearby brush that was hooked as a buck rubbed the tree. This helps to judge the width of the buck, because his antlers were hitting the tree and the brush at the same time. Bryce M. Towsley photo.

They all stress the importance of practicing shooting fast and of learning to snap-shoot. Larry says, "The boys shot thousands and thousands of rounds of ammo over the years. They just about killed all the trees here at the house by shooting into them, but that's why they are good. We used to set up swinging targets, like a nail on a string, and try to hit it on the move or throw cans in the air and hit them. If you shoot enough, that becomes easier than you might think. No matter if we were shooting 22s or our deer rifles, we try to stay with the same action design. Because we hunt with pump rifles we also usually use pump 22s or shotguns. We practice with the rifle so it becomes automatic and we don't have to think about it. We don't want to be fumbling for the safety when a deer is close. If you are on the ball and if it's not too thick cover, you have a couple of seconds when he stands up to kill him. That's not a lot of time, but if you know your rifle well and you have practiced snap-shooting until it is automatic, it's usually enough."

Lanny, Shane, and Lane are all very good skeet shooters, and that helps with the rhythm of snap-shooting. In fact, when shooting at a close buck that's on the move, Lanny sometimes doesn't even use his sights, he simply points his rifle like a shotgun.

Shane points out that, "If you don't shoot, you don't get them. I hear guys say all the time 'I waited for a better shot and didn't get it.' You have to take the first shot you are presented, but you must be able to make that shot. I once tracked a buck to its bed, it was thick and he was very close, but all I could see was his back and part of an antler. I fired three quick shots and they all hit the deer, putting him down. One bound and he would have been gone—this was the only way. If I had 'waited for a better shot' I would never have gotten that deer.

"Try to catch a buck as he stands up and have your gun ready. Sometimes they bolt right off, but usually they need some time to figure it out. That may give an extra second, but not much more. If you can see his eyes you can sometimes tell how he is going to react, but no matter what, it will happen fast so you must be ready."

Once they have a bullet in the deer they will get him anyway. With snow on the ground a wounded deer will not escape from a good tracker. Of course, no ethical hunter will purposely shoot to wound a deer, but when things are happening fast and the brush is thick it can happen. However, tracking may well be the one style of deer hunting where a wounded deer is not a disaster. These big bucks are very often worn out from traveling and rutting all night and they want to lie down. With a wound, that is only compounded and often they do not go very far. By sneaking in on his bed you can usually finish the job in short order. Shane once hit a buck on the very bottom of his foot; it laid down in 50 yards.

Our eyes are another thing that are important to train and condition to the woods. By spending the rest of the year working at our human pursuits we have already conditioned our eyes to our human environment. This is not the same as where those trophy bucks live, and we tend to look without seeing when we enter the woods. It is not easy to change the way we operate because it is so automatic and ingrained during our non-deer hunting lives.

We are trained to survive in our human environment and part of that is that we tend to watch for movement. That's what our eyes are trained for, due to the hazards of human life that pose a threat to us. For example, a moving bus will run you over and leave your carcass flat in the road, but one that is sitting still poses no threat. We are conditioned to see movement, and most deer hunters never change from that. For a stand hunter it works. There, watching for movement can be a fairly productive way to spot deer because you are stationary and they are moving. Looking for movement alerts you that a deer is traveling into your area and gives you time to prepare to shoot him. That is pretty much the art of ambushing a buck. However, when you are tracking and moving in on a bedded buck, by the time you see movement it is already too late.

The key is to learn to see what is in the woods. Learn to look for textures and shapes. Learn to see parts of a buck, the shine of his nose or eyes, the

Left to right: Larry, Lanny, Lance, Lane, and Shane Benoit and Uncle Windy in 1976.

BENOIT PHOTO

Shane Benoit "dragging one out."

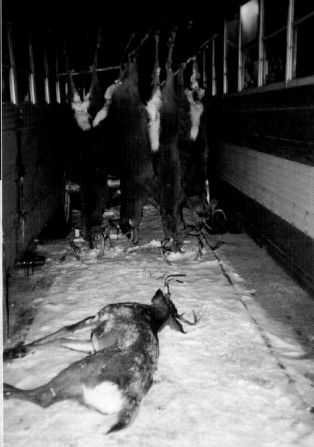

Benoit bucks from 1994.

Landon (left) and Lanny dragging out a nice buck (1988).

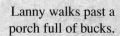

Lanny walks past a porch full of bucks.

Dick Duffy with a 15-point, 261-pound buck he took in 1993. The buck scored 190-5/8 B&C gross and they called him " Old Pot Belly."

"Good-bye my old friend, may you rest where the bucks are rutting and the snow is good."

-Larry Benoit

Shane Benoit demonstrates how quickly a carbine can be brought into play from being carried on the shoulder. The camera takes four frames a second so this is happening in a little more than one second.

In photos 1 to 5 he reaches across his chest with his left hand to grab the rifle, sliding it off his shoulder and bringing the gun around to the front. The left hand slides forward as the right hand grabs the pistol grip, bringing the gun into shooting position.

PHOTOS BY BRYCE M. TOWSLEY

Another technique is demonstrated in photos 6 to 10. As the right hand grabs the pistol grip and spins the bottom of the gun up and forward, the left hand grabs the forend as it swings up as the right hand shifts to the shooting position. The gun is mounted into the shooting position.

Shane walks down a road in a clear-cut, looking for tracks of crossing bucks.

Shane looks at a tree that has been rubbed by so many bucks over a period of years that the tree died (because of its damaged bark).

Shane checks out a buck's bed. Note the stain from the hocks on the rear leg. This helps to confirm that it is a buck. The size of the bed indicates a mature trophy buck.

Shane and Larry have a hot cup of coffee at the end of a long day.

This is a place where a buck put his head down to feed. Note the antler marks on either side which indicate a good buck.

Larry Benoit with a 250-pound, 8-point buck he took in Maine at the age of 71 (1995).

Wide, staggered spacing suggests that this is a big buck. The track indicates that his chest is wide.

Handmade knives by Larry Benoit.

Larry Benoit's Remington Model 760 carbine
showing the personalized art he applies to his guns.

The jacket patch and logo for the
Benoit's Trophy Trackers Club.

Trophy whitetails line one wall in Larry Benoit's living room.

Larry Benoit's living room: the table is full of his handmade knives and the wall showcases trophy whitetail antlers.

Painting of Leo Benoit, Larry's father, with a good Vermont buck.

A hand-painted sign illustrates the inseparable link between the Benoits and whitetail deer.

BRYCE M. TOWSLEY

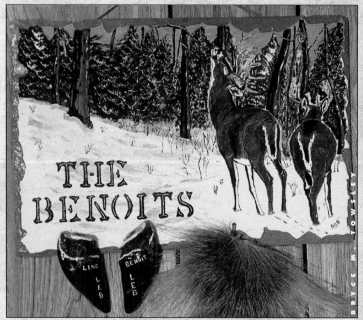

THE BENOITS

BRYCE M. TOWSLEY

Only the best are permitted to wear this patch. To earn it you must shoot a buck that has a field dressed weight of more than 200 pounds.

BIGGEST BUCKS IN MAINE CLUB

BRYCE M. TOWSLEY

Rifles and racks line the ceiling in another section of Larry Benoit's living room.

Leo Benoit, Larry's father, took this buck in Vermont in 1935. It dressed 295 pounds on a state certified scale and carried 17 points.

BENOIT PHOTO

BENOIT PHOTO

BENOIT PHOTO

Lanny and Landon dragging one across the ice.

Landon with a 205-pound, 8-point.

A truckload of 1991 bucks. There are 1,189 pounds of deer in this little truck: 268 pounds (Lanny), 268 pounds (Shane), 263 pounds (Lane), 205 pounds (Landon), and 185 pounds (Larry).

shape of part of his ear, an antler tine or a leg. Learn to see textures, to see the hair on a buck is different than the bark of a stump. An antler is smoother and different from a branch. You must be able to pick the woods apart with your eyes and positively identify what you are seeing.

One misty morning Shane saw a log that didn't look quite right. He stepped around a tree, keeping his gun on the log, and when the "log" turned into a good buck he fired. Lanny once spotted something that didn't look right and kept looking at it until he could tell that it was the white throat patch of a buck. After a couple of quick shots the deer was his.

The key is to know that what you are seeing is indeed a birch leaf and not a buck's throat patch obscured in the shade. Be certain that it is a maple sapling which simply grew at an odd angle and not the front leg of a standing buck. Is it a rock or the back of a buck's head? Is that stump in reality the back of a bedded deer? You must see and know these things before the buck sees you and is gone. All of this is radically different than what you do all year and it takes a lot of training.

It's not just the eyes that must be conditioned, but it's also the mind. If you are thinking about something other than deer hunting you will not see the deer. You must block out the distractions of life and concentrate solely on deer hunting. You cannot be worrying about getting lost, if your business partner is embezzling from you, or if your spouse is carrying on with their personal trainer. You can't be thinking about the national debt or whether you left the lights on in your truck; you must focus and concentrate on deer hunting and nothing else. All of that may or may not be important, but there is absolutely nothing you can do about it right now. It will still be there when the hunt is over and you can deal with it then. (Personally, I would already have plans laid out for the business partner and the personal trainer.) For now, though, you must focus on the hunt.

There is no time when this is more important than when you are closing in on a big buck. You simply

cannot allow a moment of inattention. You must draw yourself in and concentrate on seeing that buck before he sees you. The odds are all in his favor. You are in his environment, he sees as well as you do, smells and hears far better, and he is already focused. He doesn't have much else to do but stay alive, and if he has lived long enough to become a trophy he has at least a Ph.D. in doing exactly that. The one vulnerability he has is the rut, when he is distracted by the prospect of procreation. It is that distraction that gets a lot of trophy bucks killed and should serve as a reminder to any hunter about the importance of total and complete concentration.

Most hunters, though, never achieve it. Shane tells of one time in Maine when they found another hunter's tracks.

"We saw the tracks where a guy walked right by a bedded buck without seeing him. The buck laid there and let him," he said.

"Actually that isn't all that uncommon. Another time a guy walked into the swamp, cutting across some buck tracks. He was just walking and not trying to trail the buck. The buck was bedded off to the side and he stood up and watched the hunter. After the hunter went on by the deer laid back down. By the way, that buck died a little later," said Shane.

Again, one of the biggest mistakes hunters make while tracking a buck is walking with their heads down, looking at the tracks too much and not enough for the deer. Often hunters will become mesmerized by the track. If they would have just kept their heads up and kept looking for the deer instead of watching the ground, many times they could have taken their bucks. You can follow the track with your peripheral vision most of the time, looking directly at it only when necessary to sort out a problem.

Larry points out that we make a mistake in believing that a deer thinks like we do. "We can't think like a deer and a deer can't think like us. If we start believing that he will think like a man we will not see those deer," he said.

Larry also maintains that, "You must have your mind 100 percent on what you are doing. The

minute you deviate one little bit in your mind you will lose, because that's when something will happen and you will not be ready. Lanny has a lot on his mind with his business and other things, but in the woods he turns into a predator. He is so focused and determined that he is incredible. We used to find him miles and miles into the woods, far from his truck, often with a huge buck, because he worked so hard and stayed so focused. That's a big reason why he is so successful."

Being quiet is another important thing when you are closing in on a buck. That is one of the primary reasons that the Benoits hunt in wool.

Like Larry points out, "Wool doesn't make any noise. The synthetic stuff many hunters are wearing today is too noisy. The brush scrapes on it and it is an unnatural noise. Deer know the difference. They might hear sticks breaking all day long from deer or other critters, but they never hear a branch scrape on a ski parka unless there is a man close by."

When I was touring the woolen mills with Shane recently I was impressed with how meticulous he was about noise. We were looking at some new style non-wool shirts that they were making under contract for a mail order house. Shane used a closed ballpoint pen to rub the fabric.

"Hear that," he asked?

I barely had and said so; it was a subtle noise, one most hunters would not give a second thought.

"A buck can hear that if he is close. Lots of times when we are moving in on a buck in the thick stuff we are very close, and that is more than enough noise to alert him. Now listen to a wool jacket."

I heard nothing and again said so.

"Exactly," Shane exclaimed, "that's the point."

Larry said, "Another big mistake that many hunters make is that they overdress. They quickly get too hot and start sweating. This will throw off a lot of heat and scent. When they are uncomfortable and hot they are not paying attention and become distracted. They also make noise by breathing hard if they are overheated. You must watch loud breathing when you are close to a buck; it is amazing how far they can hear it.

"We found a lot of noise we hadn't noticed before when we started to video tape our hunts," Larry told me. "The microphone on the camera was picking up a lot of sounds that we were hearing, but not really noticing, including breathing noise. You would be surprised how loud that can become as you close in on a buck and the adrenaline starts to run through you."

Just how close do they get to these bucks? Well, Lanny once tracked a buck he didn't intend to shoot just to see how close he could get to him. He got close enough to toss his closed pocket knife and hit the buck.

It is not uncommon for the buck to know you are behind him, and as Larry points out, "They are waiting. If they can't see you, they will hear you, if they can't hear you, they will smell you." The key is to keep him guessing about your exact location. Most of the time the buck will lie still and hope you will act like most hunters and walk right by him. He probably won't move until you make eye contact or get too close and invade his "safety zone." The quieter you are and the less you move, the harder it is for that buck to pinpoint where you are and where you are going.

Larry points out that, "Some guys will fight all day long to have the wind in their face. That is almost impossible when you are on a track. You must go where the track takes you and chances are that a smart old buck will make sure that it will be downwind of him at some point. On top of that, up on the mountains and in the swamps the wind can blow in four directions at the same time. It swirls with the terrain and changes all day long. A wind on your left may be behind you 50 yards further on, so I don't pay any attention to the wind. There are a lot of deer on that wall there that were shot with the wind in their faces."

Larry points out that the buck knows you are after him most of the time: "When you are on the track the buck is often looking back at you. You have to read the sign to know when he is doing that. They get careless. They don't necessarily think like a human, and sometimes they become comfortable with you on their track. You might have been there for a while and nothing bad has happened, so they get sloppy and make mistakes.

"When we see him it's not because he wants us to see him. It's because he is in a spot he shouldn't be in. Lots of times you can see where he stopped and tramped around a little bit and you know he was looking back trying to get a good look at you. They get curious; sometimes they will backtrack to look at you. I have shot them lots of times as they backtracked. They are a curious animal, a very curious animal, even a big buck is curious.

"I was tracking this big buck one year and on the third or fourth day of tracking him I knew I had to do something different than what I was doing. He would stop and look back but always where he was too far out and in a place where he could see me but I couldn't see him. Finally I did spot him. He was out in the open timber so far he was just a speck, he didn't see me because I was still in the spruce. So I

hunched down and took off my red hat and put it on a spruce tree and wobbled it. He came to red alert, then in a few seconds I wobbled it a little more. He came a little closer, I wobbled it a little more and he came a bit closer. We did this until he was about 150 yards away, then all of a sudden he had an awful pain in his ribs.

"He would have spooked from a man, but he didn't know what the hat was. My dad taught me that trick. I used it time and time again on little bucks, either with my hat or my red handkerchief. They spook and run off and then come back. I used it one time up on Belvidere Mountain here in Vermont on a pinto deer. Usually they look, stomp, nod their head, walk sideways, and switch their tail, but they come closer. They won't always do it, but sometimes they will.

"You never know what a buck is going to do when you are on his trail. I was tracking one that dressed 235 pounds along the side of a mountain

Larry studies a buck's track (1997). Bryce M. Towsley photo.

when apparently the wind brought the scent of some does up the hill. He turned and started down that mountain just like a freight train, right to the does.

"There was a 7-pointer in his way and he hit that buck and must have knocked him 20 feet, I heard it happen. He hit the 7-pointer once, mauled him for a few seconds, and then took after the does. The does scattered and then regrouped and started down the mountain and he started after them. As for that buck he left behind, he had punched out the left eye and broken his left shoul-

Shane points out where a buck is chasing a doe that is likely coming into heat. The doe's track is splayed, indicating that she was running from the buck, which was walking. Bryce M. Towsley photo.

der. We went back a few days later and he was gone. I think he lived.

"I saw another buck one time doing the same thing. We were up on the mountain and when I saw him he was out of range. He was holding his nose up smelling for does, then he turned and came right to me. As I was dragging him out I saw that there were a bunch of does about 100 yards below me on the mountain. I suppose one was in heat and he was smelling her.

"One time Lanny and I were working our way through a thick swamp when he nudged me. There was a small buck sound asleep under a spruce tree. We watched him for a while before his eyes opened and he spotted us. He stood up and just drifted away. We didn't make any noise. Our scent may have drifted to him or maybe it was just his sixth sense, but it gives you an idea of how smart these bucks can be. He didn't bolt out of there in a rush, but more like dissolving smoke. If we had not seen him we wouldn't have known he was even there.

"Another time I was on the way to the car and I swung down off the mountain to pick up Lanny's track and there was a buck track in his tracks. That buck walked up Lanny's track for quite a ways and then cut up the mountain. I looked up and I knew where he was going to lie down, right on top of the mountain. I kept walking up the mountain and I circled to the right and up above him and I caught him in his bed. I stood there for a few minutes and watched him and he never even knew I was there. He was the fifth buck I had seen that day and I was only 20 feet from him. Actually, I have shot a lot of bucks while they were sleeping."

Lane adds to the fine points of the end game when he cautions, "Be patient at the end. Don't rush it. Those deer will hear you coming and will often wait to see you. They will hear or smell you, but until their eyes confirm what you are they will often wait and watch. You must see them first, and if you rush in you won't get the shot.

"When a deer starts feeding or meandering he is ready to lie down. If he's on a doe and she is running don't plan on him stopping, but if he is alone chances are sooner or later he will feed and lie down. That's when you go into your death creep and if you do it right it's over. But, if you blow it...!"

Larry points out that if you do blow it and the buck really wants to lie down he usually won't run very far. But that's not cut in stone and sometimes bucks will run all day.

"Usually, though," Lane points out, "they get sick of you chasing them and they get perturbed. They are used to a coyote or a dog chasing them and if they go into a brook or whatever and the dog loses the scent, it quits the chase. Well, a human being has brains enough to figure where he went in the brook and where he came back out, and to stay with the track. When that happens two or three times they get curious about what's after them. Sometimes they

haven't smelled you and they aren't sure yet what you are, but they want to find out. They know that most predators will not stay with them for that long. Sometimes they will jump sideways for 5 or 6 feet, often into brush or thick stuff to cover the trail, or perhaps they will hit a snow-filled tree and make the snow fall to fill the tracks. Many men and a lot of predators will lose them then. Some hunters will say, 'I lost his track,' but he has trampled up the place so that he can't find the deer's track. Rabbits do the same thing to the dogs. The rabbit will run in a straight line and then suddenly jump to the side. The dogs hit the end of the track and get all confused. They start milling around and scenting up the place and they lose the trail. A deer will do the same thing. A good tracker will sort it out, and when you keep

Lane with a buck that he dragged to the backside of a lake and later retrieved with a boat. He found the buck on the mountain in the background and tracked it on bare ground, killing it near the lake. Benoit photo.

times they wonder what it is that is so persistent and they make a mistake."

Remember the Benoits don't call the end game the "death creep" without reason. That reason has little to do with killing a buck and everything to do with how slowly they move. It is here that true hunters strut their stuff—and most fail miserably.

They either lack the skills or they become impatient, and either way the deer wins.

In the final analysis, it is when you have your sights lined up on that buck that you have been tracking for three days that you can truly call yourself a tracker.

Until then you are simply following footprints.

Chapter 7

Bare-Ground Hunting

"What do you do when there is no snow?"

-Heckler at a seminar

Count on it—there is one in every crowd. He's the guy who thinks he knows more than the speaker. They are as predictable as the sun rising and these guys love to bolster themselves at the expense of the "experts." During the question and answer portion of the Benoit's deer hunting seminars it's inevitable and unavoidable that some guy will stand up and look around with a smirk designed to let the audience know he is the man. He figures that he has it all worked out, he's sure that a tracker is one dimensional and easily baffled with anything less than the most ideal conditions, and now he's the guy who is going to point that sad revelation out to the world. When he has the room's attention he will call out loud enough for all to hear, "What do you guys do when there is no snow?"

Larry simply gets a disgusted look on his face that tells the audience at a glance he doesn't suffer

Left to right: Lanny, Lane, and Larry Benoit. Photo courtesy The Vermont Sportsman.

fools willingly, and with the timing of a master standup comic he leans to the microphone and deadpans, "We hunt."

Hunting trophy deer is an art that demands versatility. You can't control the weather, and snow is never a guarantee anyplace you may be hunting. Your choices are limited to two: you can hang around camp and complain about it, or you can hunt. For any true deer hunter, the choice is clear. You have to play the cards the way they were dealt to you and that means bare-ground hunting.

When conditions are right, bare-ground tracking is easier than you might think. While we were hunting together in northern Maine last year Shane pointed out a distant mountain to me. "See those ledges up near the top?" he asked. "I started a buck up there a few years ago and took him through that pass you can see and around that hill, across this

road and down into that swamp below us before I lost him when it got dark."

I sat in the truck and mentally tried to calculate the distance of that hike when he casually added, "on bare-ground."

Shane explained to me how the conditions were nearly perfect.

"It was a drizzly day with the leaves well soaked. In the hardwoods it was as easy as following a track on snow," he said. "That big old buck was heavy and he left easy-to-see tracks in the wet leaves. Down in the swamp there was a lot of deep, soft moss that was also water soaked, and it was easy to follow him there as well. Another hour and I would have gotten him."

Lane may well be the best of all the Benoits at this kind of hunting, and he quickly points out that, "When the conditions are right it is possible to track a buck on bare-ground. They still can't fly and

Shane tracked this 230-pound buck on bare ground in 1983. Benoit photo.

if a buck is moving he is leaving tracks. It isn't easy, though—bare-ground is totally different than snow tracking. You must concentrate ten times as hard and it wears you out mentally a lot quicker. At best you have only a 2 or 3 hour window to kill that buck before you burn out, so you must try to find a deer that you can work fast, one that is close. Of course that means you won't be working nearly as many bucks nor actually tracking nearly as often. Instead you will be spending a lot of time searching for a buck or track that's worth following.

"Perhaps the most important aspect of bare-ground tracking is finding and recognizing the track of a buck that you can kill. Finding them is not easy and simply driving the logging roads like you might if you were hunting on snow is not all that productive on bare ground. It is just too easy to miss the track. It's better to look on foot where you are moving slow and you are closer to the ground.

The important thing is to limit your search to the right places. There is a lot of country where you are wasting your time looking for tracks no matter what the conditions. Then, when you do find a track you must recognize how old it is and be able to make a pretty good guess about what that deer was doing when he made the track and what he is doing now. Part of that is in the tracker's art of aging a track. It takes years to learn it and you can only master it after looking at lots and lots of tracks. But the best start is to apply some common sense. Think about the weather, both now and for the last couple of days. Is the track sharp and well defined? If it is and it's raining then chances are it is very fresh. But if the edges are broken down and eroded and it hasn't rained for a couple of days you are looking at an old track. Think about the drying conditions. If it is wet and humid a track will stay fresh-looking for a long time. But if the sun is out

Lane with a buck taken on bare ground. Benoit photo.

Dave Coker (left) and Lane. Benoit photo.

Lane tracked this buck on bare ground. Benoit photo.

and the air is dry a track that is only an hour or two old may already be drying and starting to age. Mostly it comes down to thinking.

"Finding a workable bare-ground track, though, is really simple. Don't worry about traveling bucks searching for does, it's hard to find a track like that on bare-ground because your search is random. On snow you will see almost every track you pass, but on bare-ground it is easy to miss an obscure track. Perhaps there was some tall grass or hard ground where that buck crossed—you may never see his track. With those tracks, and even if you happened on one, the chances are you will never kill him. If he is traveling you can't catch him on bare-ground, and you probably can't follow far enough to catch him bedded. Instead, if you want to shoot a buck on bare-ground go to a place where there are a lot of deer. During the rut, if there are a lot of deer there is usually a big one there.

"An exceptionally large buck is a big help when you are tracking on bare-ground. Luckily, where we hunt in Maine most of the bare-ground tracking is early in the season when the bucks are at their peak weight. Later in the season they will have 'rutted off' a lot of weight. If you find a buck that is pushing 300 pounds he will leave noticeable tracks and you can follow him, but you need a serious buck to make it work well. You also have to hope he got held up somewhere by a doe or that he is lying down on the top of a mountain, because it's going to take you a long time to get there.

"I look for a big, heavy buck for a couple of reasons," says Lane. "First because bare-ground tracking is so difficult that it is foolish to put in that much effort for anything less than a great buck. It simply makes more sense to keep looking than to work that hard and to waste a day with an inferior buck. Also, I like a big-bodied buck because he leaves very definite, well-defined tracks. A heavy deer sinks in the ground more than the average buck or any doe. A big, bull-shouldered buck that has a live weight of 300 pounds or more is going to step a lot harder than a buck that weighs less than 200 pounds. To identify his track, it must be dis-

tinctive from all the other deer, as well as easy to see, that means a lot of weight and a big track. Even then it is hard to follow them.

"The buck must be close and not moving much. If he is traveling you won't get him. You simply cannot follow his tracks fast enough to catch up. It is hard enough to catch a traveling buck when there is snow on the ground, but it's all but impossible when you are tracking on bare-ground. When you are following a buck in the snow you can usually stick with him until he is ready to bed or until he encounters some does. It may be miles and miles, but so what? Following his tracks in the snow is relatively easy. On bare-ground it is much slower going and hard to follow him across vast expanses of territory because of the variety of ground you will find and the difference in how that ground will show a track. Of course, too, there is always the burn-out factor, which limits your time on the track. Any tracks are going to be harder to see than if they were in snow and you must work and concentrate harder to follow them.

"Instead, you must find a buck that's ready to bed, one that is feeding or is with some does that are ready to breed so he will hang around. These bucks are not covering much ground and you have a chance to catch them. You must be close to the buck when you first start after him because it simply takes too long to get from point A to point B. With snow you can usually just get on the track and follow it, but on bare-ground you have to work hard to sort it all out, often a few feet at a time. With snow you can look ahead and tell where he went. If you can see his tracks for a hundred yards, you have just gained a hundred yards on him. If you can see his track for a long way you can walk fast to catch up with the buck, but on bare-ground you need to look from track to track, sometimes only a few yards or even a few feet at a time and that takes a lot of time."

Even on the end game it is much harder on bare-ground because it is a lot more difficult to see the buck. There is no snow to contrast with the deer, and the buck blends in with the background. The flat gray light of November makes this even harder. The light then tends to be low in intensity, flat, and dull, which shows very little contrast. It is simply hard to see the deer and it is easy to blunder onto the buck and bump him. Remember, you can't rely on watching for movement like a tree stand hunter because, chances are if you see the deer move it's already too late. You must see the deer before he moves, and with the woods brown and gray, coupled with flat, poor light, this is tough. You have to train your eyes to look for parts of deer and to look past the brush. Concentration is important here—a moment's lapse and all of your work is for nothing. If you bump him, forget it, he's gone and you are not going to get him that day. With snow you might still have a chance, but on bare-ground the game is over and the buck won. That's why it's extremely important to kill the buck the first time you see him when you are tracking on bare-ground. To assure that you have a chance to do that you must work a lot slower and do a lot more looking when you are close to the deer. This again is slow, tedious work that will fatigue you both mentally and physically.

Lane continues, "On bare-ground the ease of seeing the track will vary with the type of ground and vegetation that he is passing through. He may be walking through the hardwoods right after a soaking rain when his track is almost as easy to follow in the leaves as it would be on fresh snow, but

Some Benoit bucks. Photo courtesy The Vermont Sportsman.

then he reaches the top of the mountain where it is spruce and bedrock. Now it becomes a lot tougher. It might be a slight scrape on a rock or some scuff marks on the ground. If you are looking for well-defined tracks all in a row you will never see that deer. Instead, you must look for the small signals that he has passed this way. If you lose the track you have to make short loops to try and pick it up again. If you can't, then go back to where you lost the track, pick up the last footprint you found, and start over. It may be that he just stepped on a hard spot, but he might have jumped off to the side. This happens frequently with bucks. Sometimes they do this to escape predators that are tracking them and you will see it often when you are tracking a buck. Most predators track deer by scent and this tactic can throw them off. A deer doesn't know that you can't smell his tracks and he may try it to get rid of you. But, if he is doing that while you are tracking on bare-ground because he knows you are after him, you are in trouble. Unless he feels comfortable enough to lie down, and it is unlikely he will if he knows you are on his trail, you may as well leave him and go find another buck.

"Sometimes, though, they are just surprised by a limb falling or something else like a rabbit or grouse spooking and it's just an involuntary reaction. The buck is startled and he will jump to the side as an instinctive maneuver to keep from being eaten by whatever it is that is thrashing in the bushes. In this situation he likely doesn't know you are behind him and you are still in business. Take note, though, that he is nervous and jumpy and keep it on your mind when you are moving in close on him.

"If he gets on a logging road or grassy spot where the tracks don't show, you just have to keep at it and don't give up. Try to think like a deer, imagine where he would travel and why. Deer usually will take the most natural path. Try closing your mind to everything and just walk where your feet take you, often you will find the track there. Years of following deer tracks will help to imprint your brain to how they think and where they will

travel. This is very helpful in following a lost track and picking it up again further along. Remember that a big buck won't necessarily go where all the other deer are going. He will avoid tight or thick places in the woods where he will have trouble getting his antlers or even his larger body through. It's sort of like trying to follow your kids, they go places you can't or won't go. Does and fawns do the same thing, they go places where a buck can't or won't go. Also, a big buck is a loner and tends to travel his own route, so it is important to have followed a lot of buck tracks to understand where he will be going rather than experience just following any deer tracks.

"Sometimes a buck will circle back to where you started, particularly if they are limited in the territory. In Maine, where they have miles and miles to travel in, they will usually light out and cover a lot of ground. At times they get headed like they have an appointment they are late for and they don't stop. But, in Vermont where the unbroken woods are usually smaller, they have a tendency to circle. Sometimes if you see this happening you can move in there and head him off. If it doesn't work out you can always go back to the track and pick it up again.

"Obviously you are more apt to encounter bare-ground conditions earlier in the season. The later it gets in the fall, the colder the weather is and the more likely it is to snow. This early season condition often means the bucks are in the pre-rut when they are scraping and traveling looking for does. If the does are still not ready to breed, a buck will usually keep checking his scrapes for indications that the does are approaching estrus. If tracking isn't working out you can try to get into a buck's main scrape line and hope you can run into him. I don't try to track then, but simply poke along on the scrape line. I prefer to stay moving and following the scrape line in the direction that the buck is moving. I like to approach him from behind because it gives me some advantage with his vision. If I am behind him and he is preoccupied with working a scrape or whatever, he is less likely to see me than if I am in front and moving at him. If he is taking time to work the scrapes and rub trees, you can sometimes catch up to him.

"Bucks will usually work the scrape line from the same direction and you can identify the direction of travel by the direction he is throwing the dirt as he works the scrapes. Usually he will approach the scrape in his direction of travel and will paw the ground throwing the dirt behind him. His tracks also indicate direction of travel, including the single, well-defined track that a big dominant buck will usually leave in the scrape. Also look at the rubs on the trees. Bucks usually rub only one side of a tree and that can indicate his usual direction of travel. He will stop and rub the tree on the side that is near him, so the rub will be visible as you approach, but on the back side of the tree as you leave. These indicators can also help you understand the time of day when he is working the scrape lines. If his direction of travel is taking him to his bedding area on top of the mountain, then it's a good bet that he is working the scrapes in the morning as he moves up the mountain to bed for the day. However, if the direction of travel is away from the bedding area, to a feeding location, or a doe bedding area, then it is probably a scrape line that he works in the afternoon as he leaves his bedding area and resumes his search for does.

"Just remember," Lane says, "during this time small bucks will often travel with big bucks. Usually it's the small buck out in front and he will go to a scrape first. So, don't shoot the first buck that shows up [unless he is big!] and be careful not to spook him and alert the big buck that may be following. If you do either one, then you have missed out on your chance for the big fella.

"When the rut is first getting started and the bucks are making a lot of scrapes, but most of the does are not yet ready, these scrape lines are great places to locate big buck in the big woods. If you are a stand hunter, simply picking a good ambush point and waiting is very effective. But, I don't like to hunt that way so I still hunt along these scrape lines. A big dominant buck may only check his scrapes every two or three days and you can hunt a long time without seeing him. But, sooner or later he will check those scrapes and if you are there waiting…it's show time!

"If the bucks are not working scrape lines it's usually either because it's too early or they have abandoned them because the does are ready to breed and they don't need them any more. When this is happening and you still don't have snow on the ground, working the trails can be effective— not just any trails, though. You can waste a lot of time with the wrong locations, so you must know which trails the big bucks are going to use. As a

Certain areas will contain "master trails" that will see use by almost every deer passing through the area. Bryce M. Towsley photo.

rule, in most places the older bucks will avoid using the same trails that all the other deer are using. But, in some circumstances just about all the deer will use specific trails in a given area. Most of the small bucks will follow those trails, so will the does, and the big bucks will use them as well. Some hunters call them master trails or primary trails. No matter what you call them, bucks will follow them from pocket to pocket of deer. Also keep in mind that the rut changes things; the big buck's behavior is different during that time than it is at any other time of the year. You can be sure that with the does using these trails, bucks will follow because if there is one thing you can count on in deer hunting it's that during the rut the bucks will go where the does are going.

"Also, because of the terrain or maybe just because they imprinted on them as a young buck learning the ropes first from their mommas and later from the older guys, big bucks will use 'master' trails, particularly in certain locations. If you look closely you can see that most of these trails have been there for years. Generation after generation of deer have used them. Land changes as do food sources, and for the deer to keep using these trails, there have to be other reasons. Usually it has to do with the lay of the land. A deer will always use the easiest route through the woods and if that means a trail that is less steep up the mountain or perhaps one that runs through a swamp on a corridor of high ground, over time it will become a master trail. These master trails actually may link with several of these locations in a loosely bound system of trails. When the going is good they will branch out into several other trails and become hard to identify, but when they encounter something like that corridor of high ground or an easy crossing at a deep stream, all those trails may link up to a single master trail for a short distance.

"I think, too, that it is something patterned into the buck, perhaps even genetically, to follow these trails. Also, as more and more deer use them during the rut they become scent trails and that too makes those big fellas follow the same path. That's not to say that every buck will follow the same trail for miles and miles, but in those certain areas there will be short stretches that just about every deer passing through will use. Usually these are in funnel areas where the terrain or physical barriers will force the deer to travel in a small area, but sometimes there simply isn't any easily identifiable reason. I suppose the deer know why, but it's their secret. If you follow these trails enough you will be able to identify these hot locations. Look for heavy deer use that will leave lots of tracks and make the trails well defined. Sometimes the trails will even be eroded deep into the earth from years and years of use. To find the best places to hunt you need to look for lots of big buck tracks. For whatever reason, some places may be used primarily by does, fawns, and small bucks. Even though you are seeing a lot of deer sign all you will likely see when hunting there are small bucks. The presence of big tracks from heavy bucks is the only sure indicator that the trail is being used by trophy deer. Also, look for lots of rubs and scrapes that indicate plenty of bucks passing through. It is not uncommon in some of these places to find trees that the bucks have rubbed year after year. Often they even kill the tree by rubbing it so much. When that happens you know that a lot of bucks are passing through.

"With lots of bucks using the trail, often you may be tracking a buck and you will run into another big buck working the same trail. If he is a good one take him. So what if he is a different buck than the one you are following?

"At times the trails peter out and other times they are really easy to see. You have to keep working on it to sort them out, but they are connected and may go on for miles. It will take miles and miles of walking to put it all together and identify these master trails and what makes them different from all the other deer trails in the woods. But, if you walk enough and watch the sign, sooner or later a pattern will emerge and it will become clear which are master trails. There really are no shortcuts in finding them other than hard work, lots of walking, and keeping your eyes open. It helps to have hunted several years in the same place because you will come to know the land well, but you can find these master trails or at least sections of them enough to hunt successfully in a single season.

"Of course, too, these are great locations for a tree stand or a ground stand if you like to hunt that way."

"Why don't you sit on the trail?" I asked.

"To be truthful, usually I fall asleep. I am just not very good at waiting. However, if a hunter can find one of these trails and he has the patience to sit there and stick with it for as long as it takes, he will kill a big buck. He will have to pass up smaller bucks, because chances are he will see lots of deer, but sooner or later he will see a big one. It's a very effective way to hunt big deer in the big country, but personally I just don't like stand hunting, so I keep moving."

Shane takes a slightly different approach and says that, "If there is no snow, you can go to where you know big bucks are crossing a logging road or other visible location and wait for them. But, I don't

really like that, so I will usually spend the time scouting—at least in the early part of the season.

"We rarely scout before the season opens. Usually we arrive in Maine a day or two before the season, just early enough to give us time to open up the camp and get things cleaned up and ready for the season. We stay for a month so there isn't really any hurry. My scouting is always done with a rifle in my hands and while the deer season is open, so technically I am hunting. Generally I will poke around in a spot for a couple of hours then try another spot. If I find a big buck, and depending on what the sign is and where I am finding it, I will often know that this is a good place to return to after it snows. But, I will try to track to hunt that buck on bare-ground as well. Shooting him now saves me all that work when it snows," he joked. "Besides, he is at his peak weight early in the season and that's what we look for in a buck, lots of body weight.

"One time I started a buck up on the mountain where we had some snow. He took me through a

Shane with a buck taken on bare ground in 1978. This was Shane's first 200-pound plus Maine buck. It weighed 207 pounds and had 8 points. Benoit photo.

grown up clear-cut that was full of thick whips and hard to see. I knew he was close so I jumped up on a boulder. The buck spooked and took off and I shot three times. The last one raked up along his side, just missing him and hit in the dirt in front of his face, turning him. If that hadn't happened and he had kept going I think I would have gotten him with the next shot.

"He ran down the mountain and onto bareground. I took him to a swamp where I was tracking in moss. I trailed him about 2 miles in 6 hours, but ran out of time and finally left him at mid-afternoon with just enough time to get back to the road before dark. It was a long walk back to the truck from there.

"I like to hunt around the edges of remote ponds and lakes, particularly beaver ponds. These are deer magnets for a bunch of reasons. Ponds are a different habitat than the miles and miles of woods that predominate where we hunt, they help to break up the monotony of the big woods and create a change. Anything that is different in the woods will attract deer. Transition lines are always good places to look for deer, whether they are between hardwoods and softwoods or between the woods and a pond.

"Ponds also create a barrier that will help to concentrate the deer movement. As a rule deer will usually not swim unless forced into the water by predators. Instead they will travel along the edge until they reach a place where they can cross. [There are exceptions; sometimes deer will swim for no apparent reason, other than they seem to enjoy it. However, they will usually choose the easiest place to cross.] Beaver ponds are particularly good for this because they can tend to be long, some-

Lanny (left) and Landon with an 8-point, 228-pound buck that Lanny shot in 1989. Benoit photo.

times filling up a good distance in a valley with a series of ponds. The bucks will parallel these, often for miles, creating good ambush sites if you like to stand hunt or good places to locate bucks."

Shane tells of a good illustration of lakes and the attraction they hold for bucks. "Another time, late in the afternoon, I found a track crossing a logging road that paralleled a lake. I went to the end of the logging road and then to the lake. There were no tracks out, so I went back and went to the other end of the lake and again found no tracks leading out. I knew he was in that block of woods and I hoped he would stay the night. I suspected that he had a hot doe in there and that I would find him in the morning.

"The next morning dawned as a rainy, drizzly day. I got on that track early and followed it in toward the lake. I found the buck in a small clearing about an hour later. He was still there feeding, bedding, and resting up from the night's activities. The only reason I saw him was that I spotted a log that looked out of place. The longer I looked at it the more out of place it looked. Finally I realized that the log was him. I took a step to the side for a better angle and saw him looking at me. I don't know why he didn't run, but it was his last mistake. I put the bead on his ribs and dropped him.

"I think that this was the buck we had seen crossing the same logging road the year before. We had jumped him out of his bed and Lanny I both shot

Shane following a road across a clear-cut. The height of the land is always a good place to look for a buck's tracks. Bryce M. Towsley photo.

and missed. Lanny stayed on the track while I went to the logging road. I caught the deer crossing the road at about 200 yards. I was all out of breath from running up there and I missed him again. His mistake was giving me another chance a year later!"

Shane continues, "I will often poke along the transition lines between softwoods and hardwoods, still hunting and looking for sign. I'll make big sweeping swings along the hardwood sides of the mountains looking for sign that a big buck has moved on toward the top to bed down for the day. I look for tracks in the leaves or perhaps a fresh scrape or rub. If I find indications that a buck has gone up the mountain, I'll go on up there and work the top in the spruce, trying to catch the buck in his bed. It's a slow, tedious process because you have no idea where the buck is bedded and you have to be careful not to spook him. Often a buck will bed with the wind coming from behind him so that he can watch downwind, while at the same time he can smell danger from behind. If it's possible it is best to work across the wind in this situation so that he has less chance of seeing or smelling you before you see him. But, if you are following his tracks you have to go where they take you regardless of the wind direction."

Larry says that if you are looking for a track on bare-ground you need to keep a close watch on the ground. It is a lot easier to miss that track than if you have snow. It may be only one or two tracks that are visible and you can easily walk by them.

"Check the high ground for sign," he says. "Each time you come to high ground you have to walk up it or across it and so will a deer, look for tracks there. A lot of times the buck will walk up on a high spot and stand there; any place a logging road crosses the height of the land is an excellent place to locate bucks. Often, as you walk along an old log road and you come to a high spot, you will find where a buck has come up out of the swamp to cross or stand there. Maybe he is trying to see better or maybe to check the wind, I can't say for sure, but I do know that bucks like these places. A lot of times you will be walking up a log road and you

will see a buck as he disappears. When you go to where he was standing it will be the highest spot on that section of the logging road."

Shane notes that doe hangouts are always good places to find bucks as the rut heats up. "Look where the does are hanging around," he says. "In cold weather a good tip is that the does will lie down on the sunny side of the hill, almost always the south side of the hill. Don't mess with them, leave them alone and circle, watching for tracks to check if a big buck has moved in to where the does are bedding or feeding. Does have food, water, and shelter and they usually will not leave unless hunters push them out. Leave them alone because sooner or later a big buck will come in to check them out. There are small bucks with the does, leave them alone too, you don't really want to kill them and if you insist on looking at them you run the risk that you will run the does off.

"If you find a track, keep circling to check if he has left, if he hasn't then try to sneak in there and find him. But be careful, there are apt to be a lot of eyes, ears, and noses that you have to get by to get a crack at that big fella."

Sometimes it's best to just wait until conditions are right. Larry tells about one buck that illustrates that point.

"We found his tracks the first week of the season when there was no snow and we were just out looking for tracks. We knew there were two good bucks and a lot of small bucks and does in this area, but we left them alone until we got some snow. Some other hunters were seeing them at the edge of a clear-cut and one kept telling us about seeing a good buck with a big rack. We knew it was the same buck from the tracks. I told that fella that with a good snow we were going after him. He thought I was bragging, but I meant it.

"Finally it did snow about a week later—only about an inch, but that was enough. It was still snowing that morning as Shane and I sat in the truck until legal shooting time. Finally we started up the mountain and I saw two small bucks before I found the big fella's track. When I did, I saw where he was with two does and that he had made a big swing to stay in the cover of the spruce edge. He had left the does, but I knew he would go back to them. I caught him walking on a logging road. He had a crippled antler that I think he had broken close to the burl while it was still in velvet. It had healed, but it wasn't a good antler. That was the side closest to me and the only one showing. It was far enough away and the brush was thick enough that I couldn't see it. I knew a deer that big had to be a buck and finally he turned to show his other side with a good antler. I shot him through the lungs, and he weighed 250 pounds.

"The point is that we left him alone knowing that he would likely stay around. We waited until the conditions were right and then we hunted him. If we had tried to take him on bare-ground, with all the other hunters watching him, the pressure might have gotten to him and he might have disappeared."

Larry goes on to sum up bare-ground hunting pretty well with this story.

"I was hunting on bare-ground late in the season one year and it was pretty tough. Then I found a buck. I saw his print in the mud and knew he was a mountain buck because he had chipped feet. The mountains have a lot of ledges and rocks as opposed to the soft moss and wet ground of the swamps. These often chip the feet of deer and when that happens it is easy to tell individual bucks. I could see his track well in the wet leaves because it was a drizzly day and he left a good trail. He had picked up a doe, but I didn't know that yet because I was still too far behind him. I followed him down an old logging road to an old camp that had a flat place bulldozed for the horses. I laid down on the berm they had bulldozed along the edges of this place and looked down through the trees. Soon I saw a movement and trained my rifle

Larry with a 10-point, 230-pound buck he shot in 1989. Benoit photo.

on it. The doe came out and I dropped my rifle and let my guard down a little. As I watched her, I saw her butt come up in the air because a buck had just hooked her. She ran and he ran right with her. It all happened so fast I didn't get my rifle back up in time and he got away.

"The next day had a fresh snow, and I picked up his track early. It was easy to identify it by the chip in his feet, and I followed it all day without getting a decent shot. The following day I picked up his track again where he and the doe played around all night. I made swings to make sure they hadn't left and then went in after him. I found him in a spruce thicket and when I jumped them I managed to separate him from that doe. He was pretty tired from breeding her all night and he would go about 100 yards and lie down. At first he was paralleling the logging road, but then he crossed. I stayed on track to the end of the spruce trees where he ran out through some open hardwood timber. The snow

had frozen and was crusty and very noisy, so he could tell where I was most of the time. But, this time he got too far ahead of me. He stopped to look back and got shot. He had lain down in the timber near the edge and in one jump he would have been gone. Instead, he stood up to look and I spotted him. I was still hidden back in the spruce and I just poked the gun barrel out of those spruce and whaled him. He was a 13-pointer that weighed 215 pounds. He had been rutting hard and was nothing but skin and bone.

"It turned out to be a three day hunt that started on bare-ground. The second day had a good wet snow, ideal conditions really, but that was the only day I didn't see him. The third day was the worst of the three with crunchy, frozen snow and that's when I finally got him. It just goes to show you that you can't predict how it will work out. Regardless of the conditions, you have to be out there hunting if you have any hope of killing a trophy buck."

Chapter 8

Bad Weather Bucks

The Benoits have certainly been written about by a number of prominent outdoor writers and I doubt there are many hunting magazines dealing with whitetails that haven't seen the Benoit name on their pages. But, what many people don't know is that Larry has some respectable credits for writing and publishing articles of his own. He wrote this one in 1985, and it was first published in the December issue of *North American Whitetail*—and it is still as relevant as it ever was.

As any deer hunter knows autumn and the deer season are a time of change. Part of the changes are the transition into winter, and the one thing of any certainty then is that the weather can be volatile.

That can be a good thing because weather changes affect buck movement. Most hunters hope for unstable weather patterns rather than long periods of clear days and high pressure. Learning to deal with harsh weather and how trophy bucks react to it can be important to any whitetail hunting strategy, and here we get a lesson from the master himself.

You will note that some themes are repeated from other places in the book, points about clothing and gear for example. This only serves to illustrate the importance of these things and how they relate to hunting in tough weather conditions. Perhaps the most important point is that a true trophy hunter is out there working and hunting, no matter what.

"To take advantage of these conditions, the first thing you have to do is to get into the right frame of mind. Forget your cold hands and numb toes and the fact that your hunting coat is lying across your shoulders like a cold sponge. Forget about everything: the wood stove, hot drinks, your friends back at camp, whether or not your car will start, whether or not you'll get snowed in. Forget about everything except one thing: bagging the biggest buck of your life."

-Larry Benoit

Good bucks taken in bad weather. Bucks left to right: 268 pounds (Shane), 268 pounds (Lanny), and 263 pounds (Lane). Shane Benoit photo.

Throughout the North and Northeast, the best deer hunting—particularly for the biggest bucks—occurs during November and December, when the weather is unpredictable. In fact, chances are it will be downright lousy. And, when many hunters wake up on the morning of their hunt and hear rain drumming on the roof or look out the window and see the snow piling up outside, they get discouraged. Wet clothes or cold hands and feet are the last things they want to put up with while they hunt.

But, you know what? I love it when I see such conditions. Of course, you don't want a downpour. But, a drizzle with a light mist is just right. Likewise, those nasty, snowy days do much to help your odds in deer hunting, particularly if you're after a trophy. I've shot my biggest bucks on days it was raining or snowing.

For one thing, you can get closer than usual, because the weather cuts down the deer's ability to see you. Snow or rain quiets the woods considerably because twigs and leaves don't crunch the way they do when it's dry. And, on wet days, scent stays closer to the ground, so it's tougher for bucks to wind you or hear you. Because they don't expect predators to be out in bad weather, deer sometimes can get a little careless under such conditions. Of course, you can't count on big bucks getting too careless, regardless of the weather; after all, they didn't get to be trophies without showing caution. Still, nasty weather does improve your odds a bit.

To take advantage of these conditions, the first thing you have to do is to get into the right frame of mind. Forget your cold hands and numb toes and the fact that your hunting coat is lying across your shoulders like a cold sponge. Forget about everything: the wood stove, hot drinks, your friends back at camp, whether or not your car will start, whether or not you'll get snowed in. Forget about everything except one thing: bagging the biggest buck of your life.

Once you've made the commitment, you need to properly equip yourself for some tough hunting. I like to track my deer, so I'm constantly on the move. Many other successful Northeast trophy hunters follow the same tactics when the weather is mean. I take particular care not to overdress. I wear a T-shirt (in especially cold weather I'll add some Duofold underwear), a flannel shirt over that, and top it off with a lightweight unlined green plaid jacket. Finally I'll add a fluorescent orange vest if it is required where I am hunting. Because I'm constantly on the move, this outfit keeps me more than warm.

But, hunters who plan to travel shorter distances might consider some extra clothing. The main point is to dress in layers so that you can shed or add, depending upon your level of exertion and the severity of the weather. The second important point is to wear outer clothing that is quiet in the woods. A "plastic" raincoat sounds like a chain saw to that big ol' buck you're sneaking up on.

Shane Benoit. Bryce M. Towsley photo.

That's why I'm partial to wool on both counts. It doesn't make noise in the woods, it "breathes," and it is the one material that retains warmth when wet. On milder days, I'll wear corduroy or denim pants, because wool gets too warm.

If you are going to hunt in tough weather, you'll want to bring along some high-energy food or snacks. Remember that tough-weather hunting can be just as tough on you as on the buck you're after. Bring along some matches and a compass as well. Be sure to take a compass reading by your car or camp before you begin hunting. That way you won't be worried about getting lost when you should be worried only about where that buck is bedded.

The snow that remains on the trees for days after a storm will coat everything trying to travel through it, including the hunter, in this case Shane, and his equipment. Bryce M. Towsley photo.

As far as the gun goes, I use a Remington pump-action rifle with peep sights. That way I don't have to worry about the scope fogging up, and so forth. Also, in bad weather, you're likely to be close to the deer anyway, so the only thing a scope can do is slow you down. When I jump a buck out of his bed, I want to be on him in a hurry. Peep sights let me do just that.

As predictable as the effects of bad weather are on hunters, they are even more predictable on trophy bucks. Of course, every big whitetail is different; they didn't get to be trophies by accident. Still, bad weather has some consistent effects on them. To start with, a big buck won't range too far during stormy weather. He'll move some, but it will be over a smaller area. Typically, he might bed, move a little to browse, then bed down again close by. This behavior applies to the big bucks of the hardwood ridges, as well as those of the lowlands.

Because a big buck will move less during bad weather, finding his tracks can be difficult. You must stay on the move. Look for him to bed down in certain types of places. He wants two things: protection from the elements and a little hump of ground that allows him to see danger. In the lowland swamps this might mean an area with a few big white pines or a big, low-hanging spruce tree. The same goes for the spruce hummocks you might find in an area of hardwoods. On the ridges where I like to hunt, I'll look for a big buck to be bedded down just over the crest, on sort of a shelf, looking down over his back track. In particular, you should watch those little hardwood hummocks ringed with spruce.

A big buck will tend to sit tight during a snowstorm and not move far from his bed. He might bed down three or four times during the same day, depending on the weather. If it stays bad for an extended period, that buck might stay in a small area for two or three days. Of course, once that weather clears, he'll be on the move again, browsing around.

This is the sort of information you want to keep logged in your mind as you hunt. So many hunters see hunting as simply walking through the woods. It's more—much more. Regardless of whether you sit, still-hunt, or track, you constantly have to be trying to outwit a whitetail by trying to anticipate his behavior. In other words, think like a deer. Otherwise, all you'll see is red squirrels and blue jays.

To complicate matters, every deer behaves differently, regardless of the weather. Every time I hunt a particular deer, I try to use his mistakes to my advantage. I note everything he does (for instance, whether or not he backtracks before bedding down). Then I log his patterns in the back of my mind, so I can increase my odds the next time. And, you have to do that too, because every time you jump that deer, he just keeps getting smarter. So, you'd better keep getting smarter, too.

Knowing the habits of a particular deer is important all of the time, but particularly so in stormy weather. An even bigger advantage in bad weather is to hunt an area with which you are familiar. Knowing the terrain not only is a safety precaution, but it should also allow you to better figure where the buck will be. It helps immensely if you have that big buck located before the hunt. Then you can really use the bad weather to your advantage.

An experience I had on a deer hunt in northern Maine proves this point. I knew of a certain big buck that consistently traveled northward along a ridge. One morning, after a heavy snow, I headed out early and took off to the east in an attempt to cut his track. I picked up the tracks and, because of the snow, I knew they were fresh. Some 3-1/2 hours later I found the deer's bed. Because the blizzard had picked up again, I was ready for him to bed down shortly; again, bad weather bucks move only short distances. I was expecting him to be nearby. I began sneaking and peeking, finally catching him nipping on buds just a short distance from his bed. I killed him with a single shot.

Still—and I keep coming back to this point—you never know what a deer is going to do until you read his sign and his track. Once you find a track in bad weather, that deer usually will be nearby. Look for short strides, places where he's nipping buds,

browsing. That deer will be somewhere right in front of you. You must go slowly—"sneaking and peeking" I call it—and try to spot that deer. It might mean getting right down onto your hands and knees in order to spot him in his bed. But, that's the way to do it, because he is low in his bed, and you are 5-1/2 feet tall or more. It can help to team up in bad weather. Sometimes, my son Lanny and I will hunt the same deer. I'll read and follow the track, while Lanny, who's got really sharp eyes, walks parallel to me. He stays about 5 to 10 yards off to my side and just keeps his eyes peeled for that big buck. One of the reasons we are successful at this is that we intuitively know what each other will do, having developed this over many years.

Of course, nasty weather can make the tracking difficult, depending upon how hard it's snowing and how much snow is on the ground. So, it can be hard to find the track. The snow can be blowing hard up on the ridge tops, and you must be able to distinguish that big buck track in 6 to 12 inches of snow.

When we get a foot or so of snow and it's still snowing, we'll zigzag the ridge tops, looking for that track. Remember, the track will be filled with snow, but don't think that that necessarily is an old track. Given the way big bucks behave in bad weather, that deer could be really close. Remember, their pattern is to get up for a while, browse, then bed down again.

During a snowstorm, be sure to zigzag, keeping your pattern short. Remember, the nastier the weather, the more likely that deer is to sit tight in his bed. I once shot a big blizzard buck that had less than a pound of food in his belly.

For this reason, bad weather means you generally will have better luck moving, even if you prefer to sit in good weather. The deer simply don't move much then, so stalkers and trackers will end up seeing the most deer. I'm a tracker, so I like to keep on the move anyway. Also, tracking allows me to select the deer I want to hunt. The sitters don't always have that option. But, the point is that during nasty weather, regardless of your in-

clinations during nice weather, stalking and tracking make the most sense.

There's one important point to remember about tracking in bad weather: it might be hard work, but the chances are the deer is very close to you once you hit the track, and if you take your time, you can get even closer still. Of course, this is difficult; the same conditions that allow you to get close to the buck make it hard for you to see him well. It makes it hard to maneuver, to keep your poise, to keep your confidence high. You must believe you'll see a buck any minute; otherwise, you'll never see any. The fact that I've shot my biggest deer in snowstorms helps me keep this confidence level.

Sitting can pay off if you are near the bedding area of that big buck when the weather breaks. Particularly if it has been raining or snowing for a while, the bucks will be on the move once the weather clears. The dominant bucks will be traversing their home territory.

Like any other wildlife, deer make allowances for mean weather. So, next time it begins raining or snowing when you pull into camp, don't become discouraged. Make up your mind to hunt all that much harder.

When you come right down to it, the truly "tough" weather days are those crisp, clear mornings that provide the backdrop for calendars and pictures of big deer. I know that many hunters consider these good weather days the time to be hunting, but not me. I like my hunting when the weather is the worst, because I know that on such days my chances of bagging a real trophy are at their best.

Chapter 9

Hunting with the Benoits— A Lesson in Deer Hunting

"It was amazing to witness their ability to "read" a track as well as I can read a book."

-Bryce M. Towsley on hunting with the Benoits

It was snowing hard as I turned off the paved road and I took that as an omen for a good hunt. Snow that is fresh each day is a gift to a tracker, a gift I hoped was following me to Maine. I knew it had been a tough year so far, with a warmer than usual fall and a lack of snow until just a few days ago. There had been a winter kill, the deer population was down and reports coming out of Maine were not all that good. It was getting down to the wire, the fat lady was warming up and running the scales. This was the last week of the month-long deer season, the week I would be hunting and I hoped that things would turn around.

The unplowed road that passed through those wild and uninhabited miles was rough, snow-filled, and narrow. The bridges were single lane and narrower, the rivers they spanned cold, dark, and uninviting. My map was crude and my directions a bit vague, my penance for forgetting to make a call before leaving on another trip. Miles in, I found what I thought was the turn onto an even narrower road with deeper snow and far fewer tracks. I passed an open gate that I expected to be locked and that kindled a growing doubt if this was the right road. I knew the dangers of making a mistake. As a northerner with a wandering spirit I have spent more than a few hours with stuck trucks that had been taken farther than they should have been. Nobody was expecting me this night and there would be no rescue if I found trouble. In this part of the world a mistake could be disastrous.

It was well past dark when after a few more miles I turned around and headed back for the gate. I was going to check the lock to see if the combination that Shane had given me would work and confirm that this was indeed the right road. Halfway back I met a truck with Vermont plates and as we passed on the road I waved him to a stop.

I could tell by his hesitation in answering my question that the driver knew where the Benoit's camp was. They no doubt are bothered by a lot of hunters who want to visit when they want to sleep, and a friend keeps his secrets. I was about to explain that I was invited when from the darkness of the passenger side

1997 bucks. Benoit photo.

A Maine river. Bryce M. Towsley photo.

Shane (left) and Lanny with Lanny's 1997 buck. Benoit photo.

came a familiar voice. It was Lane Benoit's, hailing a greeting that changed everything.

"Follow me," said the driver as he started off.

I did a tricky 3-point turn and tried to keep up. A mile past where I had given up and turned back we made a right and a few yards down a hidden lane were a couple of old school buses that I recognized from a hundred photos.

The first thing I saw when walking from my truck to the closest bus was a big 9-point whitetail buck that was stuffed into the back of Lanny's Suburban. I hoped that it was yet another omen of a good hunt ahead. In the bus, Larry and Shane made the introductions and I started my first week of whitetail deer hunting with the Benoit family.

I knew that I was fortunate in that I would be experiencing something that many deer hunters throughout the country could only dream about. There are no lack of good people who would want to hunt with this legendary family, but it was me who was sitting at the table. Furthermore, I was here not just to hunt, but to learn. It was my time to study under the masters, to try to unlock some of their secrets, and to pick their brains for the next

ten days. It was a powerful thing when I thought of it in those terms. Here I was with the very guys that are idolized by millions, with the hunters that I grew up reading about, that we all tried to emulate. I knew that in these buses were likely the four best whitetail deer hunters alive. For a man such as myself, who has shaped his life and livelihood around deer hunting, it was a humbling experience.

The spell was shattered, though, when after a plate of beans and hot dogs, Larry growled, "Get your stuff and grab a bunk, I'm going to bed. Turn off that light and try not to make too much noise."

They weren't too much on formality, and to be honest I liked it that way. It was clear that I was part of this, a member of the hunting party for the week—much more than a guest. I was expected to hold up my end of things and to be part of it all, not as an outsider or a writer in the way as he tried to find the words for a book, so much as a hunter. As I slid into my sleeping bag and tried to find the sleep I knew would elude me that night, I smiled at the darkness. This was going to be fine.

I am not a morning person and I was still groggy and disoriented when what seemed like only sec-

The depth of Maine's cold is reflected in these bucks. Benoit photo.

onds after my feet hit the floor somebody said, "Let's go." I stumbled out of the bus to see taillights disappearing down the road. The cold that greeted me was oppressive, cold you could taste, cold you could feel, a brittle cold that anchored the unprepared, and I was pleased when my old truck started at the first turn of the key. I pulled it into gear and tried to catch up. Breakfast was a chug of what little orange juice I could thaw in the truck's heater and a couple of granola bars, gulped down while wrestling the truck down a four-wheel drive road at warp speed.

Right after daylight we passed a clear-cut with a big cow moose feeding in it. She looked very black against the snow and very large. Moose may be more common in this part of Maine than whitetail deer. While the habitat and climate of this place is less than ideal for deer, the moose thrive and prosper here. The up-side is that only the toughest deer survive and through nature's selection process there have evolved some of the largest whitetail deer on earth. Live weights of 300 pounds are not uncommon on a mature buck. For the northeastern hunter who gauges his trophies by the field-dressed weight of the buck, this may be the promised land.

There are not many deer and most hunters find this a frustrating place to hunt. I would find out later that during this same week a friend of mine was hunting nearby with a well-known and *reputable* outfitter where he spent 63 hours in a tree stand without seeing one deer. Few hunters can find consistent success with big bucks here and those who do are trackers like the Benoits.

Not a mile later a much bigger moose, this one a bull, jumped out in front of Larry who was ahead of me and started running down the road. He was a good moose, perhaps the bull of the woods, but I didn't think so. One side of his antlers was broken off, likely from fighting during the rut now two months past, leaving a stub that stuck out past his ears while the other antler that spread out far from the left side of his head was wide, flat, and carried uncountable points. I would like to see the bull that was powerful enough to twist off his antler—he, I

think, was the top dog. The bull ran down the road in front of the trucks for nearly half a mile before he finally jumped off to the side and let us pass. It was a show worthy of an appreciative audience, which it had. Already this morning was showing some of northern Maine's best.

We drove on for miles, some back on the paved road and a lot more on yet another remote system of logging roads. When we finally stopped Larry and Shane were out before my truck stopped rocking, and were looking at a huge buck track.

"This is where Lanny shot that 9-point yesterday," Shane explained to me. "There must be a doe in heat in there because there were a couple of other bucks hanging around and now this one has joined the party. Lanny is going to take the track. Why don't you grab your rifle and jump in my Bronco with Pop, we are going to try something a little different today."

Larry loads his clip in preparation to start on a big buck's track. Bryce M. Towsley photo.

As we drove Larry explained that Lanny was going to get on the track of that buck to get him moving, while the rest of us converged on that section of woods from different locations.

"Everywhere we hunt people follow, and because we have been coming here for several years there is a lot of traffic on the roads," Larry explained. [I hadn't seen another truck all morning, but I would later learn that it doesn't take much traffic to alert these deer. They are used to quiet all year, and when a few extra trucks show up and start spending the days prowling the roads, the bucks that have lived through a few hunting seasons take notice.] "Most hunters don't wander far from their trucks and damn few will go into that mess that Lanny just headed for. It's too thick and nasty. The deer know that and that's why they are in there. They are also very road-wise here. That buck yesterday took Lanny and Shane 'round and 'round this section of woods, but he would not cross any of the logging roads. He just kept circling and twisting back on his own tracks. They covered miles and miles, but never left this woods. [Of course that "little patch of woods" was probably 5 square miles.] That buck he's after today will probably do the same thing, so we are going to cover some of the trails and escape routes. We will try to pick up his track ourselves to gain some time and ground on him. So, if you find his track get on it and pay attention."

As Larry predicted, the buck stayed in that patch of woods all morning. Actually, there turned out to be two bucks that were over 200 pounds in there and neither wanted to leave. It was bitter cold that morning and the snow was crunchy and noisy. The storm from the night before had been short-lived and dumped only an inch or two on top of the frozen 6 inches that had already been on the ground. While that made for easy conditions for following the tracks, it was extremely noisy. Lanny said later that the deer listened to his steps and stayed just far enough ahead to not be seen, never working harder than they needed to stay alive. In that thick jungle of whips, blowdowns, and spruce, that sometimes meant only a few yards separated the hunter and the hunted.

"More than once I could hear the buck walking, but I couldn't see him," Lanny said. "I figured that would happen and that's why I took his track. With that buck yesterday my ticket is punched and I can't hunt anymore, but I knew that the guy on the track had the poorest chance of seeing the buck in these conditions anyway. Instead I would keep him moving while the rest of you try to cut his track."

The cold was taking its toll; we had to keep moving or freeze, and the buck could hear us walking as well. It was just too thick and too noisy. Finally about noon we called it a draw and headed for the warmth of the trucks.

Nobody said much as we ate and tried to thaw frozen body parts. But, then the heaters and the sandwiches worked their magic and soon enough Shane suggested we go look at some new territory.

Larry (left) and Shane look at the tracks of a big buck that crossed the road just before daylight. Bryce M. Towsley photo.

"I tracked a good buck through here a few days ago," he said as we walked down a faint trail through an old clear-cut. "I want to show you something he left behind."

About a half-mile into the clear-cut Shane turned left and started down a deer trail. It turned out to be one of those spots that are perfect, a trail on a little high ground that spanned a swamp and connected two old clear-cuts that provided food and shelter for the deer. The trail was short at this point as the two clear-cuts almost came together, with perhaps 100 yards between them. It was only this little bit of swampy land, sure to mire any vehicle, that kept it free from the tree harvesting equipment. The trail ran on a thin section of ground that was just high enough to stay drained and dry. This was clearly a travel lane for bucks seeking company with the does and fawns that were feeding on the new growth in the clear-cuts. I remember thinking that a hunter would do well to put a tree stand up overlooking it and to stay with it until he killed a buck, which was a likely thing to happen.

"Look at this tree he rubbed," Shane said to me.

"It's dead. Why did he rub on a dead tree?" I asked.

After looking a little closer and with a little instruction from Shane, it became clear that this tree had been rubbed on by a lot of bucks for a lot of years. There were old scars that healed and fresh ones that never would. The bucks had rubbed so much on this tree of perhaps 8 inches in diameter that they had ruined the bark all the way around and killed the tree. Still, though, they continued to rub on it. Sure there were lots of fresh rubs on other trees in the area as well, but it was obvious that they still were using this tree too.

"This tree has been used by bucks for years and years," Shane told me. "It is a sign post for deer and every buck that passes through here will rub on it a little. They become so used to rubbing on it every time they pass by that it becomes almost instinctive to them. There have probably been generations of bucks that have used this tree. I suspect that they were traveling though this spot even before these

clear-cuts were made. This is just a natural travel corridor for them. It makes a great place to pick up a big buck track."

"Or put up a tree stand," I added.

"I suppose so, if you *have* to hunt that way. Isn't it boring?"

That night we feasted on deep-fried alligator meat that was from a 12-footer I had taken on a bow hunt in Florida earlier in the fall. I cooked it on the gas stove in Larry's bus, served it on plastic plates, and we washed it down with half-frozen Cokes. Our appetites were sharpened by the long day and the energy-burning cold, and I think that was as fine a meal as I have had in all my travels.

The Benoit camp consists of two old school buses that they have converted to campers. The very rear has four bunks, two top and two bottom. Close by on the right side is a cast-iron wood stove, opposed

Shane prepares some lunch in the school bus that is the Benoit camp. Bryce M. Towsley photo.

by a set of shelves for food. There is a sink in about the middle of the bus on the left side, along with a four-burner gas stove. Next to the stove is a bus seat turned to fit against the outside wall. Across from that is a table with a bus seat on each side. There are a couple of gas lights, one over the sink and another over the table. (Lanny's bus, which is parked beside this one, is similar with a few variations in the layout.)

It gets crowded, and diplomacy and patience are required for several men to live in this bus. If one is standing, then the others must be seated. Only one person can move about comfortably at a given time. This can create some friction at times and hilarity at others, but usually it all works out.

The bus has little insulation, and on these cold late-November nights you will find that anything left on the floor is frozen. It is cold sitting at the ta-

ble, requiring that you keep your boots and often your jacket on, but the sleeping area, which is closer to the stove and slightly elevated so it serves as a collection point for the rising hot air, can be sweltering. One night I found that my black sleeping bag, which was on the top bunk near the roof, had absorbed so much heat that it was too hot to touch. The stove burned down later and by morning the -20 degree rating was a godsend.

With that bunk being the collection point for all of the heat in the bus, one night it was too much for me to take. It was so hot I couldn't breathe. I climbed down, but sitting at the table I was cold. I made a couple of attempts to get back in the bunk and sleep, but it wasn't working and I was sure that sooner or later I would wake up Larry and Shane. As a guest, that was the last thing I wanted, so I put on my boots and emptied out the camper shell on

Inside Larry's school bus. Left to right: Lane Benoit, Dave Coker (with face hidden), Lanny Benoit, Milan "Cobb" Lawson, and Shane Benoit (with back to camera). Benoit photo.

the back of my truck. With all of my gear piled on the ground behind the truck I threw my sleeping bag in the back and tried to get a little sleep before morning. The temperature went down near zero that night and suddenly I wasn't hot any more.

"You didn't snore at all last night," Shane said when he got up. "It was great."

After that I moved into Lanny's bus where there was a lower bunk available. It went pretty well except that Lane, who was above me, was less tolerant of my snoring and would pummel me a bit as I slept. I mentioned that I was probably keeping them awake and perhaps I would move back into Larry and Shane's bus.

"You stay right where you are," Larry told me on no uncertain terms.

I wonder why?

There is no running water in the buses, only the woods for an outhouse, and no hope for a shower. The interior heats up fast in the morning by simply turning on the gas stove to assist the wood fire and cools down fast at night when the flames burn down. It could well be the epitome of a deer camp and in a word it's a great camp to hunt deer from.

I have been lucky to have hunted deer all across the U.S. and Canada and I have experienced hunting camps of all types. They range from one on Anticosti Island in Quebec where I was often met at the door in the evening by a maitre'd in a tuxedo who presented me with a glass of champagne and a cracker with caviar on it, to the other end of spectrum that would likely be the camp I started bow hunting from. It was nothing more than plastic sheeting nailed up around some trees with a roof of scrap metal and a dirt floor.

I felt more at home in the plastic camp. Somehow it always seems like I am more of a deer hunter, a

better predator, when I am at the more rustic camps. Perhaps it is a repressed memory of my early years at our family camp, or maybe the memory goes back even further to a fur-clad ancestor who hunted to survive. Either way, I am most at home in a rough, but comfortable camp, and these buses fit that nicely.

The next day was Sunday, and Maine's antiquated blue laws forbid hunting then. Still, we were moving shortly after daylight. Larry, Shane, and I traveled the lost logging roads for miles, looking for tracks, scouting the country, and trying to see what the deer were up to. It was truly amazing that seemingly every new vista, every mountain we passed, and each swamp sparked a memory of a buck that they had tracked. They have hunted this part of Maine for about 9 years, but the stories sound as if they had a lifetime invested in the place. Many times we would stop to look at tracks and I would "go to school" as Larry and Shane instructed me in the fine points of identifying the track as a

Lanny with some 1990 bucks. Left to right: 220 pounds (Shane), 185 pounds (Landon), 225 pounds (Larry), and 255 pounds (Lanny). Benoit photo.

buck or doe and in judging the size of the deer and the age of the track. It was amazing to witness their ability to "read" a track as well as I can read a book. It is for many a foreign language that is used to write the story, but as they explained things and understanding slowly came, it was as I might envision learning French to be.

By afternoon we were back at the camp installing new sights on Shane's rifle. I had brought them with me for him to field test, and after re-zeroing the rifle I decided to check my own gun. Finding it fine, I broke out my 7600 in .35 Whelen and proceeded to shoot out the screw that was holding the target. Knowing when I am ahead with a gun, I put it back in the case, all the while noticing that Larry was watching.

Larry reminds me of my own grandfather with his old-time Vermont accent and inflection on his words as he talks. As with my grandfather, that accent became more pronounced during hunting season. That similarity was strengthened after I broke out my .44 Magnum and Larry indicated the same disdain for handguns that Gramp harbored. Like my grandfather he grudgingly accepted its capabilities when I managed to put all of my bullets in the bullseye. I hoped that at the same time I had scored some points in proving to him that I could shoot a little. Somehow that seemed important to me.

Near dark we headed into town to eat. The options are limited in this rural area, but the restaurant served a good ribeye steak. I only wish I had ordered it. The seafood I had instead was tasteless and sog-

Maine law doesn't allow hunting on Sunday. Sitting around the fire are (left to right): Larry, Lanny, Landon, and Shane Benoit. Benoit photo.

gy. I suppose I should have known that a restaurant that survives on loggers, truckers, and hunters is going to have better beef than fancy seafood.

This also was the time to gas up, stock up, and make a phone call home. It was amazing that everywhere we went in this little hunting-oriented town people recognized Larry Benoit. Here, close to Quebec, it was not uncommon for them to use the French pronunciation of the name, but regardless they recognized the man—not only on this night, but each time we stopped here or in other towns to gas the trucks or buy a loaf of bread. No matter if it was the gas station, the store, restaurant, or even the local bar which harbored the town's only inside pay phone, people recognized him. Larry is reluctant to accept this fame and is, I think, a little annoyed and puzzled by it all. His standard line when someone asks if he is "Larry Benoit" is to say, "Naw, my name is Smith and I ain't seen a deer all season."

Most don't buy it. They know this is the guy they have been reading about all of these years and they just laugh. Some take offense and a few even think that they made a mistake. They all want to talk deer hunting. One guy insisted that I had to be Larry's brother and that he could see the family resemblance, particularly in the chins. I am not too sure that I like the implications. Not that I mind being mistaking for a Benoit, but I am 33 years younger than Larry! I know it's been a tough year, but it shouldn't show that much in my face!

I suppose that the years of this sort of celebrity have worn on Larry, who really just wants to hunt deer and be left alone. He certainly recognizes that with his fame comes this sort of thing, but 30 years is enough—it's time to pass the torch, let the next generation field the questions and sign the autographs, his dues are paid.

Just after full daylight on Monday morning, I spotted a deer at the top of a clear-cut. I stopped the truck and backed up to see a big bodied deer running off. I caught up to Larry and Shane and told them that I was going to take the track. We agreed to meet later in the day, but it wasn't to be. I

wouldn't see them again until after dark and then it was back at the camp.

I returned to find the track and saw that two deer had been feeding and bedding at the top of a clear-cut on a steep side hill. I took the track and I was not out of sight of the truck before I realized that I was overdressed, even though I was wearing far less than I usually hunt in. I should have listened to them, but after Saturday's ordeal I added an extra layer with a heavy sweatshirt. Today was warmer and the terrain much tougher. This was a shirt that I would soon start to hate personally as I dogged this track through some incredibly thick and steep Maine real estate.

I judged the tracks to be a doe and a buck of about 170 pounds. Not a trophy by the standards we are using, but one I would take if I found him this way. I based this assessment on not only the tracks, but on the beds. The larger of the two had

The towns in northern Maine are small. Note the population of The Forks. Bryce M. Towsley photo.

stains in the snow where the tarsal glands would be and that coupled with the larger, blunter tracks left me thinking it was a buck. His foot wasn't as big nor nearly as blunted at those giant tracks we had been seeing all week. He didn't have the flat-footed walk of a big buck nor the broad stance of a wide-chested deer, but still I was certain it was a buck and worthy of a chase. They didn't run far before slowing to a walk, which I took as a good sign and picked up my pace a little, trying to close the gap.

I followed for perhaps a mile before the doubt started. There was no doubt now that one was a doe, because when she urinated in the snow there was one small hole melted away and centered between the tracks. But, that other track was making me wonder. At times it looked like a good buck, even larger than I judged it to be, with a big foot and a heavy step. At other times it looked smaller and not even a buck for certain. The tracks took me through brush that I could barely ram my 220 pounds through, and some that I had to go around.

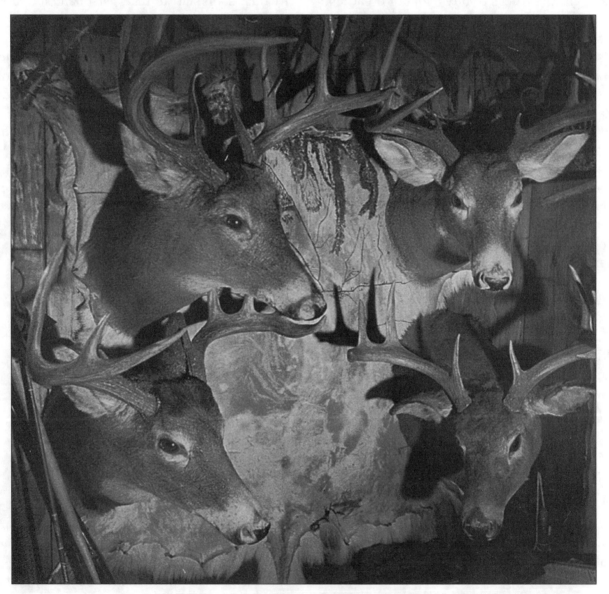

Larry Benoit's mounts, set in the position they were looking at him when he shot them. Photo courtesy The Vermont Sportsman.

Certainly, if it was indeed a mature buck he wasn't carrying much for headgear or it would never fit through this stuff. Sure, he could make it go if he had to, but these deer were not in a hurry and didn't have a clue yet that I was behind them. They showed no indication of slowing down and were obviously ready to travel. I figured from the beds and the tracks that they had been resting for a while and now it looked like they were willing to cover some ground. Each time I debated on how good a buck I was following the thought grew a little more that, if I had these questions, it probably wasn't worth spending too much time on.

Then the track turned down the hill and skirted the landing of a log road. A quick look at my compass indicated that it was the road my truck was parked on; a check of the GPS confirmed it. The deer had made a big circle, and I was now less than a mile from my rig. The decision at that point was easy. I wasn't going to spend that much effort on a questionable deer. If I had found them quickly I would have tried to shoot him, but it was evident that they were not going to make it easy and he certainly wasn't worth a 20-mile hike. I turned down the road.

At the truck I noticed that my left glove was missing, gone from my jacket pocket and somewhere back on that mountain. A further check of my equipment showed that my new fiber optic front sight was broken, perhaps when navigating some of the thickest brush. Things were suddenly going wrong, but I knew that as soon as I got in the truck and had some lunch they would get better. Yeah, right!

When I tried to drive ahead I discovered that while it looked fine when I pulled in, I had picked a poor place to park. The wheels spun on the snow-covered ice and the truck slid down the bank to the woods. Within a couple of minutes I was hopelessly stuck. The truck was up against some small trees with the wheels over a big rock. I couldn't move the truck an inch and "rocking" it out had ceased to be an option. The nearest tree behind me was across the road and too far for my chain and come-a-long to reach.

I spent the next hour jacking the truck high enough to install tire chains. Because of the angle of the bank, each time that I got it about high enough the truck would slide sideways and off the jack. By the time I got the truck back on the road and everything put back in place it was mid-afternoon. I had a sandwich while the heater tried to dry my soggy clothes and I went looking for Shane and Larry.

I found out later that that they had left and gone to some new country where Shane was on a good buck. For now, it was evident that I was on my own. I used this time to learn the road system

Lanny's Suburban crossing the river. Bryce M. Towsley photo.

in this area and to look for a larger buck to pursue tomorrow.

It didn't matter that I found nothing exciting, because I went with Lanny and his son Landon the next day. Lanny is fast about everything he does and that includes driving. He flung his Suburban down those remote logging roads like it was an Indy race car. All the while he looked for tracks along the road. For most he slowed down and for many we stopped. But, at times he would judge them without letting up on the gas pedal. I was amazed at how fast he could judge what he was looking at.

Shane checks out a fresh scrape found while tracking a buck. The height of the overhanging branch worked by the buck would indicate a big deer. Bryce M. Towsley photo.

"What about that track we just passed," I asked?

"You mean that big old doe?" Lanny replied with obvious surprise that I didn't know that.

I wasn't even 100 percent sure it was a deer track.

We drove for miles before the road ended at a wide river. Lanny barely slowed down as we plunged across. It was cold and the river looked dark and uninviting, like a giant flowing cauldron of some vile and oily liquid well-laced with ice chunks. Ice flows built up and bounced off the side of the vehicle as we drove through the swiftly flowing river, and I wondered if there was a buck big enough to be worth risking being swept downstream to the Atlantic Ocean miles away.

"The water dropped a bit during the night," Lanny commented. "Yesterday it was high enough that it was coming in the doors. My little boy here almost got his feet wet," he joked. (Landon is well over 6 feet tall and far from little.)

Just as we climbed the bank on the far side of the river we encountered a big mud hole that was frozen over. The ice was 3 inches thick, but not enough to hold the big Chevy. We broke through and had to work back and forth in the water that was again almost to the doors, breaking a few more feet of ice each time, until we could climb out 50 yards down the road. Before I had a chance to comment we were into another mud hole and again playing icebreaker.

"Are you sure this is worth it?" I asked.

"Yup, we found some big tracks in here yesterday," came the reply with no doubt in its voice.

We looked at least half a dozen tracks that I would have taken. But, Lanny would get out, follow them for a few yards and then be back in the truck and rolling just that fast.

Finally he took a little longer on one. "This is a track that interests me," he said. I was still looking it over trying to see why when Lanny and Landon walked past me, Landon with a rifle in his hands.

"Take the rig. Just pick us up on one of these roads this afternoon," Lanny said over his shoulder as they disappeared into the woods, looking for all the world like a couple of hound dogs working a hot trail.

When we hooked up again hours later I was amazed at the distance these two had traveled in the time they had been in the woods. Lanny explained that while the buck had left a big track, it had fooled them.

"When we finally found him I don't think he weighed 185 pounds," He said. "He just had big feet. He was a young buck and if he grows up to fit his feet he is going to be a great trophy in a few years."

Another day, Shane and I followed a buck for several miles. He took us through a 4 year old clear-cut that showed evidence that he had traveled there often.

"This is part of his travel route," Shane said. "Look at his tracks and you will see that he has passed through here at least three other times in the last week."

I kept it to myself that this would be a good place to sit in a tree stand. With these old clear-cuts, a good approach is to find a tree along the edge and get up high. If you use an accurate, flat-shooting rifle and make sure you have a rest for it to shoot in any direction, you can cover the clear-cut pretty well. With a good pair of binoculars, warm boots, and a lunch a patient hunter could do well. While I knew that Shane wouldn't hunt that way, to be honest it didn't appeal to me all that much that day. It was too cold.

From there we traveled into a spruce swamp where the buck had stopped to make a scrape. His tracks indicated that he was a good buck, but the height that he was breaking off branches over the scrape indicated that he had a good high rack as well. I noted that and Shane said, "Yes, you are right, but I already knew that the rack was tall."

"How could you tell that," I asked.

"Remember back near the edge of the clear-cut when he ducked under that big log. His chin marked the snow while the top of his rack scratched the bottom of the log. In looking at the distance between the ground and the log it was clear that he was pretty tall."

We followed him for quite a while in the swamp until he turned and crossed the road into another older, clear-cut. We followed him along the edge where he kept to the woods, only a few yards from the more open clear-cut. Then he turned and walked out to a small knoll that was covered with small maple whips.

"He'll bed there," Shane whispered to me. "He can watch his backtrack, and when anything following steps out of the woods he can be gone before you know he is there."

Sure enough we found his bed on top of the knoll, right where Shane had predicted we would. He had vacated it some hours ahead of us, pausing to rub a tree near the bed. The large bed was stained from his tarsal glands, but the buck smell was faint. We guessed him to be a few hours ahead of us (well all right, Shane guessed, I just agreed).

When he turned some time later and crossed yet another road we knew we were gaining ground. We had checked this road before we started on his track and he had not crossed then. This pinpointed more closely the time he had on us. We had been on his track for about 2 hours, so he had to be less than that ahead of us.

He took us into yet another swamp where we found lots and lots of deer tracks. One set was from another buck that was at least as good as the one we were following. As the tracks criss-crossed and doubled back while mixing with each other, a variety of doe and I am sure other, small buck tracks, until it became hard to stay with the buck we had been on. We considered that either buck would be fine, except that we knew how much time this buck had on us, with the other we didn't have a clue. Better the devil you know as they say, so we made our best effort to stay with the buck we had the time invested in already.

Shane was methodical and patient when the tracking became tough. He would stand and study the tracks, puzzling out "our" buck.

"It's important not to walk in the deer's tracks," he told me. "You don't know for sure if you have to come back here to start over and you don't want to step on any of the tracks and wipe them

out. Stay to the side of them and be careful where you are walking.

"Look here where the two bucks crossed tracks. See how the one we are following has pushed a little snow into the other tracks? That means that these tracks are fresher than the others. They had to be there when this buck came through for him to knock that snow into them. See, too, how when the buck drags his feet he is plowing up little miniature snowbanks or little ridges of snow. Look how when the tracks cross, this buck's ridges are slightly rolled over the top of the ridges from the other buck. That means that these tracks were made last. We are after the fresher buck track."

We took that buck on for a while more through a swamp that was incredibly thick with spruce, willow, and maple whips. It was full of deer sign, more than I had seen anyplace else during this week in Maine. It was clear that this buck was traveling and looking for does. He had probably rested up in the bed we had found and he was ready for a night of debauchery and partying, or least what passed for partying for a whitetail. We were more than a week past the peak of the rut and most of the does had already gone out of estrus. He obviously wasn't finding what he wanted here and he obviously was going to keep on going on until he did. He seemed to know all of the hangouts for the local does and he took us through some places that were obviously holding pretty good deer populations. As he did, I found more and more places that I knew a dedicated stand hunter could take a good buck. There were many places where trails crossed and intersected and on each were tracks from good bucks in the old snow. Although they were varied in age, it was clear that the deer moved freely here in this thick and remote area.

Finally, by mid-afternoon, we both came to the conclusion that we were not going to catch this buck this day. We sat for a while and had a snack while we went through the ritual of debating the question that we both already had answered in our minds. It was time to leave this buck, declare that he had won this round, and make our way back to the road.

A quick check of my Garmin GPS brought pleasant news, because we were actually less than a mile from the last road we had crossed. When we hit it, planning a long walk to my truck, we had yet another pleasant surprise. Larry was coming down the road with Shane's Bronco. With all of the talk these days about guardian angels, I could almost believe in them. It was as if mine knew how spent we were and was looking out for us. I made sure to whisper a quiet thank you and remind him that we still didn't have a buck.

"You know," Larry said around a mouthful of mashed potatoes that evening, "I have hunted with a lot of writers over the years. I remember one who was taking a lot of pictures while we were tracking a good buck. He kept talking about 'shooting' this tree or 'shooting' that track. We came up over a ridge and there was a little spike horn buck standing there. I pointed to his camera and asked if he wanted to shoot that little fella.

"Before I knew what was happening he grabbed my rifle and killed the deer. I was on the track of a huge buck so he had to drag that one out by himself. We were a long way from the truck too.

"That fella went on to become quite well known nationally as a writer and editor of a big magazine. 'Course it was a fishing magazine."

He went on, "Another time I had a fella out with me who was asking a lot of questions about deer sign and how I could tell so much from it. I found a fresh pile of pellets that the buck we had been following had just left and I explained that knowing what he had been eating would help us find him. I pick up one and pretended to put it in my mouth. I chewed a bit and told that fella I could taste birch and beech browse. I chewed a little more and mentioned beechnuts and raspberry bushes. Then I spit out a gob of chewing tobacco on the snow, which looked pretty realistic. Before I knew what was happening the other fella picked up a handful of pellets, put a couple in his mouth, and started chewing.

"He said that it tasted pretty bad and that he couldn't tell anything about what the deer was eating. Trying not to laugh, I told him he wasn't paying attention, that it takes practice, and to keep chewing a little longer."

The reluctant direction-giver in the truck that first night turned out to be Dave Coker, a good friend of Lane's. In fact, Lane was the best man at Dave's wedding. His wedding present to the couple was a deer head. He had the antlers from a good buck that Dave had shot in New Hampshire mounted using a cape from Shane's 268-pound buck.

"He said he was going to get me a fishing pole," Dave told me, "but he knew he would break it so he got the deer head mounted instead."

Dave has been hunting with the Benoits for 17 years and he says that they have definitely influenced his hunting style and philosophy.

"It's funny how it takes a natural progression as you go," he said. "It's not something I knew was happening, it kind of snuck up on me over the years. When I started hunting in Maine I just wanted a buck, it didn't matter too much how big it was as long as it was a legal buck. But, now I hunt only trophy bucks, 200 pounds or bigger.

"It was definitely my association with the Benoits that made me a better hunter by making me more aggressive. I grew up hunting at a camp in Vermont and I was always taught to go and sit to wait for a buck. I killed some small bucks that way, but I didn't like it much. Once I started hunting with Lane and had some success it made me more aggressive. I started going out and getting the bucks instead of waiting for them to come to me. In the first years Lane and I did a lot of double teaming, where he stayed with the tracks and I did the shooting. I learned a lot and it sure changed my thinking about deer hunting. Now we go our own way when hunting and usually I hunt alone.

"I work hard to stay in shape so I can hunt hard and I learn more every year. I don't think you can ever know it all, but each time in the woods teaches me something. I was saying to Lanny the other day that by the time I learn enough to be really good at this I will be too old to do it.

"I have learned a lot too by coming back every night and listening to the stories. With five guys in the woods tracking deer each day, every night somebody has something that I can learn. Probably the hardest part has always been knowing when to go fast and when to slow down. Anybody can charge ahead on a deer track and overrun the deer. They may even get a shot, but the secret is to know when to slow down so that you can get in on the buck and kill him."

When I arrived there Dave had a buck hanging that he had shot earlier in the season. I asked him about it.

"He is the second buck I have taken off that same spruce knoll in 2 years. I shot him less than 200 yards from where I got the buck the year before.

"I had hunted this area for a while, and the bucks always seemed to go to this same place to bed. In 1996 I was following a good buck and he did the same thing. When he turned I thought, he is going to run right up on the knob again, the same as last year. The deer always wind me, and by the time I get there all I find is beds. So, this time I circled around and behind the little mountain and went up over the top with the wind right in my face. I got within 10 yards of him before he came out of his bed and I shot him.

"That buck weighed 225 pounds when I got him the last Friday of the season. It was late in the year and he was rutted out pretty good with very little fat on him. He was a big-framed buck that would have weighed a lot more earlier in the season.

"That trick worked again this year. It was snowing and the wind was blowing hard. I was following a buck and a doe track that were pretty blown in and hard to follow, even though the tracks were fresh. Then I cut another track that was smoking fresh; the buck had to be right in front of me. The hardwoods there are wide open, you can see for a long way and the wind blows across those hardwoods and up on to that spruce knob.

"These deer were headed up there. I was pretty sure that they would stay for a while so I circled around and came over the top again, keeping the

wind in my face. The first indication that they were there was when I heard antlers hit together. It was pretty thick in there, all blowdowns and Christmas trees, and the two bucks had clicked heads trying to get through. That got my attention so I turned and saw them. They were only about 25 yards at that point and at first I didn't think that the one I could see best was all that good as he ran away from me. The other one was a small-ish 6-point, so I turned my attention back to the bigger deer. Finally he turned broadside at about 80 yards. I could see he was at least 200 pounds for sure so I shot him. He didn't have very big antlers, but he dressed 207 pounds."

Thursday was Thanksgiving and in celebration Shane and I decided to go into town that night and get a shower at one of the truck stops. Before we did, though, we stopped at a local restaurant. The place was full of people and we failed to notice the closed sign in the window.

The lady explained that this was her family eating and that this was their holiday dinner. We apologized and started to leave when she called us back and insisted that we "go in the kitchen and grab a plate." We politely protested, but the smell of the fresh roasted turkey was too much to resist.

Later the woman refused our payment and acted a little hurt that we even offered it. She may not know it, but that little act of kindness to a couple of rough looking (and rough smelling, I am sure) deer hunters did a lot to restore my faith in humanity. It only reinforces my deep belief that the places where hunting is still important are the places where the last good people are living.

Like any good week always does, this one passed all too quickly, and by Saturday at noon I decided to start on the long drive back to my home in Vermont. True to form, Landon and Lane both came in that night with big bucks, taken on the last day, in fact the last afternoon of the season.

For Lane this is common-place; he has a well-deserved reputation for taking big bucks on the last day and even in the last hours of the season. I should have realized that and stayed to work the cameras the following morning, but I had been on the road for nearly two months and was, I suppose, a little homesick.

I am often asked about hunting with the Benoit family. I can hardly sum it up with words, but if forced to, I would have to say that it was in every way an adventure, a learning experience, and a treasured memory.

Dave Coker with a 218-pound, 8-point buck. Photo courtesy Dave Coker.

Chapter 10

Equipment—
What Works, What Doesn't

"Everything we carry is for hunting deer and nothing else."

-Larry Benoit

In the years since the hunting world was first introduced to the Benoit family's style of hunting, one of the most identifiable and drastic changes in the deer hunting industry has been in the equipment. New fabrics and materials have changed clothing and footwear, new rifles and calibers have hit the market, and certainly scopes have become much more commonplace. Trends and preferences have also changed how we look at and choose the equipment we hunt with. Our clothing has become a fashion statement as much as it is pragmatic. So, too, does our other equipment make a statement, and many hunters feel they need the newest rifle

design, chambered for the hottest new cartridge and topped with the latest technology in optics.

Of course, there is a practical side to all of this: there is little doubt that great advances have been made in the equipment we use. Gore-Tex was a word nobody knew 30 years ago; the same for Thinsulate and Cordora. Stainless Steel rifles with synthetic stocks were unthought of, and cartridges such as the 7 mm STW or the .30-378 Weatherby weren't even a dream. These have all changed the face of deer hunting equipment, and much of it has helped to make us more comfortable and better hunters. Few of us still use the same equip-

1991 bucks. Left to right: Lanny, Shane, Lane, Landon, and Larry Benoit. Benoit photo.

ment we did in 1970 to hunt deer, but the Benoits are the exception. The equipment they use has changed very little since that time. The only concessions I can see are that the Jones-style hat is now in blaze orange and has been coupled with an orange vest. This is primarily to comply with Maine law, which requires blaze orange in both a hat and a vest. Larry has upgraded his gloves a little from the inexpensive brown cotton ones he used to use, but that's about the extent of it. Everything that travels with them into the November woods is pretty much the same as it has been for three decades, or maybe longer. It is not that they are unaware of the new advances, it is simply that for their style of hunting and the region where they hunt there is nothing that truly improves on what they have been using all of these years. Their equipment may well be the epitome of the old saying "if it ain't broke—don't fix it!"

Nothing extra is carried and everything must serve a function or it is left behind. At first glance it would seem that they take so little into the woods with them that it would make a Spartan sob and beg for mercy, but such minimalism is not without reason. A frivolous pound or two in the dawn's early light may not seem like much then, but 20 miles and 10 hours later you will learn to hate it personally. Weight, or the lack of it, is important and a minimal amount of equipment is how they achieve that goal.

There is little doubt about the influence of the Benoits on hunters in the Northeast. Green plaid jackets, rubber boots, and Remington pump rifles are as common in the north woods as blue jays. Many hunters no doubt bought these to emulate the Benoits, but they soon found out that the Benoits use this equipment with good reason—it simply works.

Because they are constantly on the move and covering so much ground in the course of a day, they dress extremely lightly. A tree-stand hunter wouldn't last the morning before hypothermia claimed him if he dressed like the Benoits. But then if they dressed like a stump sitter and tried to track

a buck they would likely collapse from heat exhaustion within the first mile. It's all a matter of hunting style and what works.

The tendency is to overdress, and I quickly recognized this when hunting with them. The first buck I tracked was on a cold, bitter morning in late November. Thinking that the thin wool jacket would never be enough, I added a sweatshirt under it. I hadn't gone a 1/4 mile before I was sweating. If you think you are dressed too heavily, you are. If you think you will freeze, you are just about right. Walking on a deer's track all day consumes a lot of energy and that converts, at least in part, to heat. A sweaty hunter is not only wet and uncomfortable, but is also in danger of hypothermia.

In spite of the incredible multitude of offerings in fabrics for hunting today, the family's backs are still covered with green plaid wool jackets. The choices vary little, and Larry and Shane prefer an unlined jacket with a double shoulder. The "cape" that forms the double shoulder covers across the back from about the shoulder blades on up and down an equal amount in the front. It acts to help to shed water before it can soak in, as well as increasing warmth without adding bulk and weight. They don't like backpacks, and because this jacket does not come with a game pouch in the back like some other models, they will sew in a pocket along the bottom in the back to hold their lunches. Lanny, Landon, and Lane prefer a lightly lined jacket that comes with a game pouch which they use as a place to store lunch, etc. Like Lane says, "If I am heading out at daybreak I want lots of food. We all carry a lunch in the game pocket of our jackets." This jacket is lined in the back with cotton chamois cloth that adds warmth and helps to wick away moisture.

The Benoits know that wool is still the warmest and quietest fabric for deer hunting in the thick north woods. (Incidentally, thousands of Northeastern deer hunters agree on this point.) It remains warm even when wet, which it will be a lot when hunting in the Northeast where the only sure bet about the November weather is first that it will surprise you and second that it will sooner

or later turn nasty. Wool is an excellent insulator and is fairly light in relation to the warmth it provides. Furthermore, it is very quiet in the woods. This last point is extremely important. While easing through the woods the fabric must be able to have branches brushing against it without making any noise. That means no noise at all, for even what we might figure as insignificant can spook deer. A buck has incredible hearing and any noise you make will not escape his attention. You may get away with snapping a branch or crunching a leaf because these are natural sounds, noises he hears all day as other deer, squirrels, and birds move around in the woods. But, you will not get a second chance with a noise such as a branch scratching against nylon because it is a sound that is not natural to the woods. A cagey old buck will

Larry Benoit on a buck's track in 1997. Bryce M. Towsley photo.

know the difference and be gone. When you are closing in on a big trophy buck, clothing that is "pretty quiet" is not enough—it must be completely silent. Most synthetics simply cannot do this, even the best are too noisy to meet the tough standards that the Benoits demand. Other than wool, cotton is about the only thing that comes close, but it is a poor insulator and is worse than nothing when it's wet. Wool is the only thing that meets all of the requirements for noise and protection from the elements. Surprisingly, even after decades and perhaps centuries, this fabric still meets them all very well and with no real compromise.

The jackets are in a green and black checked pattern which has become a trademark of sorts for the Benoits. They chose it primarily not as so much as an identifier, but for more practical reasons.

"I prefer not to be seen in the woods, either by the deer or other hunters," says Larry. "The green check jackets act like camouflage, helping us to blend in. We don't worry about getting shot. We hunt in remote and rugged areas where other hunters don't want to go. We hardly ever see another hunter in the woods and when we do we'll usually see them first and avoid them. Also, we know that anybody who is hunter enough to be back in as far as we hunt is going to know what he is doing. Good hunters know what a deer looks like, they don't shoot at something they shouldn't be shooting at. Of course Maine law now requires blaze orange so we are more visible than we would like when we hunt there, but you have to follow the law."

They will wear only a light flannel or chamois shirt under the jacket, usually without an undershirt. Their pants are jeans or light weight wool pants, depending on the weather. If it is really cold they might put on a pair of Duofold long johns, but it's got to be pretty bitter before that happens.

Their feet are the primary mode of transportation and they will put on a lot of miles in the course of a deer season. If there is a single most important piece of equipment it may well be their boots. If they can't walk they can't hunt. It's really that simple. They hunt in a harsh environment; Maine is not a nice place in November, with snow and cold a promise. The terrain will vary from steep mountains with rocky ledges to vast swamps with lots of moss hiding buried cedar roots.

The miles and miles of walking day after day will take a toll on the feet, so good boots with a good fit are important. At the same time, it is crucial that they can move quietly through the woods. This places a great demand on their boots. For a lot of years the Benoits used uninsulated rubber boots from a well-known manufacturer, but they recently made a switch to Sorel brand boots, which they feel are a better design. Most of them prefer the unlined Saranack model rubber boots, while Lane likes an insulated boot that's a little higher and wears the Widgeon model. I froze my feet years ago and have trouble keeping them warm. I like the Manitoba model, which is a light rubber boot with a thin removable felt liner. These boots are still very

light, much lighter than other felt-lined boots and they are completely waterproof. They are not for sitting on a stand in cold weather, but they are a little warmer than the unlined boots and are great for this style of hunting. I wasn't in camp very long before they caught the attention of Shane and Larry, whom I suspect will each have a pair by next year.

Regardless of the model, the important point is that the boots fit extremely well, almost like a shoe. There must not be any slipping because that will soon lead to blisters. Also, a tight fit insures complete control over how they place their feet on the ground, something that is extremely important to moving through the woods quietly. Remember though, that perfect fit is important, but this is a fine line because boots that are too tight will restrict circulation in the feet and they will soon be cold.

The sole must be flexible and soft so that they can feel where they are putting their feet down

These uninsulated rubber boots from Sorel are important to the Benoit hunting strategy. Benoit photo.

when they are approaching a deer. The boot must be able to transmit the feel of a stick underfoot before it breaks. At the same time it must also provide reasonable protection from the cold, wet environment of the Maine woods in November. The tread design is also very important. Traversing the side of a mountain in 6 inches of fresh snow with the wrong boots can be a lesson in frustration. The sole must provide traction while the boot gives stability and ankle support. When they are 10 miles from any road and twice that far from another person, a fall could be a disaster. Being dressed as lightly as is necessary for tracking and probably being sweaty from exertion, when combined with an injury, can lead to hypothermia very quickly.

Larry notes that, "We always keep a change of clothes in the car. We never know what the day is going to bring and we are liable to be miles and miles from the camp. If you get back to the truck and you are wet you can change and keep hunting."

Larry makes their knives. It's a tradition that started when his father made Larry's knife for him back when he was 13 years old, using black diamond steel to make the blade. His dad was a blacksmith, and this tough steel used for wagon wheels and sled runners made a wonderful knife blade, which Larry finished grinding and assembling. He got into some trouble with his father for taking a piece of brass for the handguard without asking. The brass was from a disassembled scale being repaired for a customer and was an important part of the scale. But, that didn't deter him and he has been making knives every since. He sells most of them, but each member of the Benoit family uses one of his knives when hunting. The blades today are made of high carbon steel. They are 3-1/2 to 4 inches long with a leather-wrapped handle and a brass finger guard. They are housed in a strong leather sheath that protects them from the razor sharp blade. The knife is carried on a leather cartridge

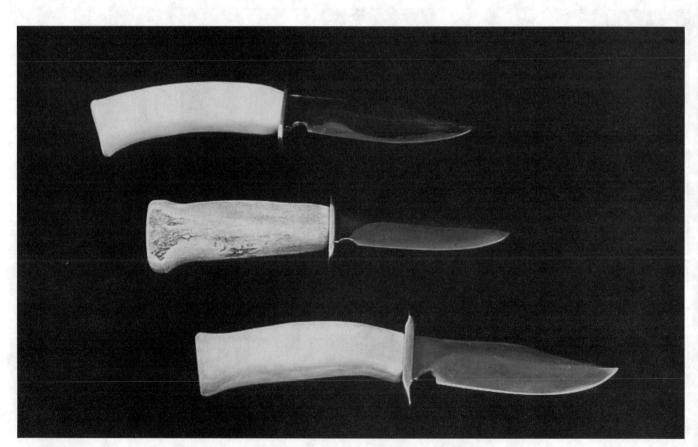

Handmade knives by Larry Benoit. Bryce M. Towsley photo.

belt that will have an extra twenty or so cartridges in the loops. They are adamant about having plenty of extra ammo, and this is one of the few places they will compromise on additional weight. While it's rare that they shoot that many rounds at deer, it is not uncommon to have to shoot to signal for help with a downed buck or to help a hunter out of the night woods.

Sometimes, though, they do a lot of shooting. Lanny is prone to "gattling" with his rifle and he will almost always shoot more than once at a buck. "It's more fun that way," he says with a grin.

The cartridges are carried in the belt instead of a pocket for a couple of reasons. One is that a belt distributes the weight evenly around their bodies and makes the load less noticeable. The other is that cartridges in a pocket will tend to clink and rattle against each other. Once again, this is a foreign noise in the woods and will alert the deer. The same might be said for coins in a pocket—you may

not think they are making much noise, but a big buck may disagree, so leave them at home or in the truck. If you wish to carry a coin for a pay phone, put it in your wallet or wrap it in a handkerchief. But today, even that is unnecessary because any phone will accept credit calls.

A length of drag rope, usually plain old vanilla nylon clothes-line rope, with the ends burned to keep it from unraveling and measuring about 5 feet long, will also be on the cartridge belt.

This remote country can become featureless in a snow storm or on a foggy day so, although they rarely need it, they all carry a compass with them. Any good woodsman will have a sense of where he is at any given time. He will be subliminally aware of the sun, wind direction, and the multitude of other things that keep him oriented in the right direction. But you cannot depend on that when conditions change. If it is snowing, foggy, or at night, for example, your mind can trick you. Larry once

The empty casings as they fell after Shane finished shooting at his 268-pound buck. Benoit photo.

Shane works on his equipment belt inside the school bus that is the Benoit camp. Bryce M. Towsley photo.

Shane takes a compass reading. Bryce M. Towsley photo.

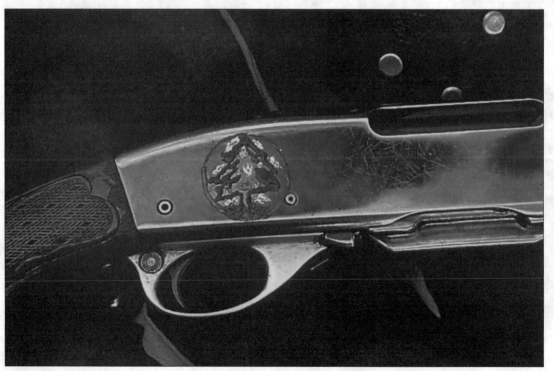

Larry Benoit's Remington Model 760 carbine showing the personalized art that he applies to his guns. Bryce M. Towsley photo.

mentioned in print that he relies on the compass in his head.

"I really wish I had never said that," he told me. "Too many people misunderstood. I carry a compass and I recommend that every hunter carry one."

Lane says, "I always carry a compass, I learned that I can't always rely on the one in my head. Usually it's all I need, but once in a while I need a compass. Sometimes the fog comes in and you can't see from here to there. Other times it's snowing so hard that you can't see. Without a compass you are in trouble. There are some places in Maine where I don't recommend anybody go without a compass. The way the land lays it plays tricks on your mind and you can get lost. One minute the brook is going this way and then it's going the

other way and you can get lost. You can't walk a straight line in the woods without landmarks and if you have a day with low cloud cover where you can't see the landmarks or the sun you need a compass. Because you are always trying to find an easy way through the woods and because we all favor one leg over the other, you will walk in a circle if you aren't careful."

Larry notes, "The places that Lanny hunts you need a compass. If he gets on a straight line he will take you to the mountain and beyond."

Shane and Landon are both using GPS units and have found that they are great for a lot of things, not the least of which is navigation in the woods.

"They are also great for getting a handle on how far apart things are," said Shane. "Sometime when

A Garmin GPS unit. Photo courtesy Garmin.

Shane takes a reading from his GPS. Bryce M. Towsley photo.

If possible, it is always a good idea to rest on a tree to shoot. Bryce M. Towsley photo.

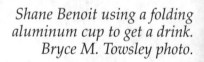

Shane Benoit using a folding aluminum cup to get a drink. Bryce M. Towsley photo.

you have to drive miles and miles of road to get to another spot you don't realize how far it is from where you just came. With the GPS we know at a glance. We also have used them to mark downed bucks, or even where we left a track at dark. I use mine a lot for scouting and to mark places I want to come back and hunt. If Pop had a GPS back in '81 he would never have lost that big buck up on the Norris Branch and probably wouldn't have spent the night in the woods. But of course, they weren't even invented then." (See Chapter 11)

The Benoits carry aluminum cups that fold flat to fit in a shirt pocket and pop open to form a cup. When there is snow on the ground and along the banks it is tough to get your face down to a stream to drink without getting your shirt wet. These cups work great; you can stand up and drink, which is much more comfortable.

Aside from the green jackets, the Benoits are most identified by their rifles. They exclusively use Remington pump-action rifles, Model 760 or the newer 7600, in .30-06 or .270 Win. Although the Benoits have no formal connection with Remington and have never been offered free guns or anything else from the company, I'll wager they have sold more pump-action rifles than any ad campaign ever devised. They are incredibly popular in the Northeast and that is due a great deal to the fact that the Benoits use them. I know that my own 760 .30-06 was bought way back in 1974, long before I ever knew the Benoits, but I bought it primarily because Larry used one like it. Even these days, when

1997 bucks. Benoit photo.

I can basically use any rifle I like, it is still that battered old .30-06 that I take when it's time to get down to business.

The Benoits prefer the shorter barrels of the carbines, however, and Remington currently offers the carbine only in .30-06. If the gun is a full-length barrel (22 inches) such as on the .270 Winchester, they cut the barrels down to 19 inches. The shorter barrels handle better in the brush and they feel that they swing better on running deer. The small loss in velocity from the shorter barrel is not important as the majority of their deer are shot at relatively close range.

They modify the rifle stocks, cutting down the comb until their dominant eye is precisely behind the rear sight and shortening the length of pull, until the rifle fits them perfectly. They replace the hard rear buttplate with a recoil pad. This serves several purposes. First, of course, it reduces felt recoil for the shooter. Also, the rubber pads will stay in place on the shooter's shoulder when mounting the gun and while shooting. Finally, it seems like a small point, but the rubber pads are quieter in the woods. If you set the gun butt down on a rock when you stop for a breather, the noise of hard plastic may be enough to spook a buck. Rubber is silent.

The Benoits try to fit the rifle much like a custom shotgun so it fits perfectly with the individual shooter. These modifications are particularly important for snap-shooting at running deer, when the gun must be mounted quickly and has to be pointing at the same place the eyes are looking when it hits the shoulder. A slightly shorter stock insures that the butt will not snag on their jackets as they mount the gun, while at the same time it forces them to bring it back against their shoulder, which positions the eye and head for shooting.

For years the height of the stocks on the Remington pump-action rifles was just about perfect for

The author's "Benoit" rifle, a Remington 7600 carbine in .30-06. It is fitted with a Williams peep sight, a Williams "Fire Sight" front sight and sling, and swivels from Uncle Mikes. The ammo is Remington 180 grain round nose Core-Lokt. Bryce M. Towsley photo.

shooting with iron sights. The reality, though, is that most shooters will put a scope on their guns these days and the stocks were changed. The newer 7600 rifles have a higher comb designed for use with a scope. Iron sights put the shooter's eye closer to the line of the barrel than does a scope and these stocks will be difficult to use with either peep or open sights. That point was well illustrated to Shane, who bought a new rifle in 1997. He had the barrel on the .270 Winchester cut down to 19 inches and a recoil pad installed on the stock, however, he left the comb as it was shipped from the factory. He experienced some problems when trying to get off fast shots while hunting. He found that, because the comb was too high, he was searching for the sights instead of having them pop up right under his eye.

The solution, of course, is to modify the stock by shaving down the comb with a rasp a little at a time, continually trying the rifle until it is right.

While this makes for more work, especially considering that you will likely have to refinish the entire stock to make it look right, the end result is a rifle without compromise. The fit will be as perfect as if you had a custom stock maker build it for you. You will find that if you do it right, the rifle will hit your shoulder and the sights will be in perfect alignment in front of your eye.

My own "Benoit" style rifle I put together to hunt with them is a Remington 7600 carbine with an 18-1/2-inch barrel. Because this is currently offered only in .30-06, and also because of all of the calibers recently chambered in the 7600 (with the possible exception of the .35 Whelen), the .30-06 is my favorite, I had little to fault with that chambering.

I fitted it with a Williams peep sight. These are designed to screw into the two rear scope mount holes and are quickly installed. I replaced the front

Tests conducted by the author with a variety of shooters and on all rifle action types have concluded that for aimed repeat fire the pump-action is likely the fastest and most reliable. Bryce M. Towsley photo.

sight with a Williams fiber optic "Fire Sight" and installed swivels from Uncle Mikes, making sure to place the rear swivel stud far enough forward to allow cutting down the stock for a recoil pad. Although I ran out of time before the hunt, I have a 1-inch pad, also from Uncle Mikes, that will be installed after hunting season. I cut down the comb until the sights were in perfect alignment with my eyes. While I sealed the wood with some stock finish for now, I think I may paint the stock camo when I have the gun completed.

This gun is a great shooter, better than I had ever hoped it would be, particularly when shooting with a peep sight. But then, all of my Remington pumps have been good shooters, although I have to admit that some needed a little more tinkering than others to get there. This little carbine was one of the easy ones.

On the Benoit's rifles, the actions are slicked up and polished until they work as smooth as glazed ice. They want them to be fast for any repeat shots. The triggers are adjusted to break cleanly and crisply at about 3 pounds.

Why a pump? Semi-autos are faster for sure, but only if the goal is to make noise. For speed of fol-low-up shots, no action style is even close to being as fast as a semi-auto, but when shooting at a deer or any other target the pump has the advantage. The simple motion of pumping the gun helps to speed up the follow-up shots. As the slide is brought back to eject the empty shell it assists in bringing the gun down out of recoil and as it is slammed forward with a fresh shell it will bring the gun back on target. If the hunter keeps his eyes on the deer as he works the action, the motion of slamming the slide forward will naturally bring the barrel and the sights back into alignment with where the eyes are looking. For aimed fire, most experienced shooters will agree that the pump is faster than any other rifle style. When tracking deer this is an important feature in a rifle. Often the shots you must take are fleeting as the bucks are running though the thick brush. It's hard to make every shot count, so a speedy second, third, or even fourth shot is important. Of course, the goal is to kill him with the first and only shot, but the reality is something entirely different. Often it takes more than one shot to bring down the buck, and the speed at which you can aim and fire those shots is crucial to your success or failure.

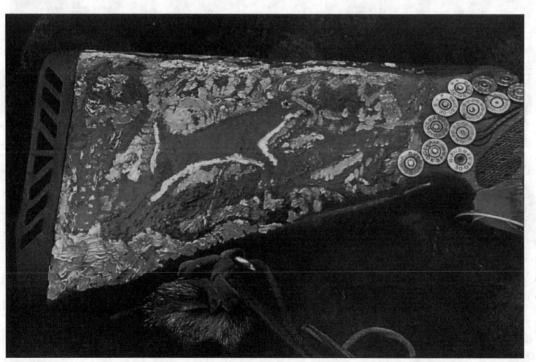

Larry Benoit's Remington Model 760 carries a deer's ear, which honors the buck's hearing and elusiveness. Bryce M. Towsley photo.

Semi-autos are also heavier and more prone to trouble. With the ice, snow, mud, and cold of deer hunting in the north country sooner or later most of them will malfunction. The pump has the advantage of more power to open the gun when it is covered with ice or full of mud from a fall. They are simply more dependable.

In reverence to their Iroquois Indian heritage, some of the Benoits decorate their rifles with symbols, talismans, and remembrances of bucks past. Simple art is painted or carved on the receiver or the stocks and on some of the rifles they have the head of any shell casing that killed a 200 pound plus buck inlaid in the wood. The problem is that with any rifle they have owned a while there is simply not enough room for the casings of all of the bucks they have taken with the rifle, so often they stop adding them before the gun is completely overwhelmed. (We should all have that problem!)

"We also honor the buck," said Larry. "We have a tradition to keep the spirit of the deer with us. We do this with a piece of a buck's ear on the gun. It serves as a talisman, but it's also to keep the spirit of the deer with us on the hunt. Because a deer hears better than any animal in the woods, our Indian ancestors tied a piece of a deer's ear to their bows for good luck. We keep one on our rifles for the same reason. We honor the majesty and importance of these trophy whitetails and this serves as a constant reminder of the deep love and appreciation that we have for the animal that has been so important in our lives."

The rifles are loaded with Remington 180 gr. Core-Lokt factory loads in the .30-06 and 150 gr. Remington Core-Lokt factory loads in the .270s. They use only round-nose bullets because they feel they plow through the brush better than pointed bullets. (Incidentally, an extensive test I did for *Deer & Deer Hunting Magazine* a few years back confirms this. I tested a wide variety of cartridges as well as bullet weights and designs. After firing hundreds of rounds through "brush" under carefully controlled conditions, my conclusions were that bullet shape was likely the single most impor-

tant factor to how well a bullet tracked after contacting brush. The round nose design did the best of all the bullets tested.) Also, the round nose bullets transmit more shock to the deer than the pointed bullets because they have more initial frontal area. They are already larger at the point of contact than pointed bullets, so they start transmitting energy sooner and have less "expanding" to do to reach full mushroom. These big, tough, winter-conditioned bucks have an incredible tenacity to life. Trophy bucks are really in a class all their own in toughness when compared to other deer, and it is important to use a caliber that is powerful enough and a bullet that is heavy enough to insure that you can put them down quickly. Because most shots are close, 150 yards or less, the poorer aerodynamics of the round nose bullets are not a problem. Even at 200 yards the difference is much less than most hunters think. With a 100-yard zero the 180 grain .30-06 round nose bullet drops 5.5 inches at 200 yards. With the same 100-yard zero the 180 grain pointed bullet will drop 4.8 inches at 200 yards. This is less than a 1 inch difference, and very few hunters can shoot well enough to have it be a factor.

All of the rifles wear a simple sling, which they use for carrying the rifle. The gun is kept on their shoulder most of the time, being taken off when the sign tells them that they are getting close. They leave the sling on the gun, but Shane says that sometimes when the brush is thick and he knows he is close he will hold it in his hand to prevent it from catching on the brush.

None of the Benoits use a scope on their rifles. They shoot well enough with iron sights that they don't feel it is necessary. It snows a great deal during November in Maine and even if the snow is a few days old it will cling to the trees and brush so that you are constantly covered with it as you move though the woods. A scope can plug up with snow and fog over at a critical time. It can be a heartbreaking situation to see the buck you have been after for days long enough for a shot, only to find the scope full of snow when you try to sight through it. You

wipe the snow off, but the glass underneath is fogged with moisture, and then the buck is gone. With iron sights there is less to clog up, and if they do, you can simply blow or brush the snow off the sights. Also, Larry is quick to point out that a scope adds weight to the rifle and can upset the way it carries. Both are important when hunting involves miles and miles of carrying the rifle.

They usually replace the factory front sight with a high ivory bead front sight so that the bead floats above the barrel when aiming. Then they paint the bead red for better visibility against the snow, although with the new Williams fiber optic "Fire Sights" front sights, this is no longer necessary. These sights gather ambient light, will actually glow orange, and are very visible under a variety of light conditions. Shane and I tested them in 1997 with excellent results. The one concern was durability, and the jury is still out on that. Mine was an

early model that had the fiber optic protruding from the steel sight about 1/64 of an inch, and it broke off on the second day of hunting. The sight was still very usable and still very visible, though, and I hunted the rest of the season with little complaint. Shane had a newer sight on his gun that has the fiber optic tight to the steel sight, and there were no problems. Because he prefers an open rear sight he also used the fiber optic rear sight Williams markets as the Remington Sight Set. Shane says he likes the sight picture very much with the three glowing dots all lined up and thinks that this may be the best open sight he has tried. I think that fiber optics will replace painted beads as the Benoit sight of choice quite soon.

The rear sights on their guns are usually Williams peep sights. They remove the insert, leaving a big, easily visible hole to sight through. This is accurate enough and allows them to follow a running

The Williams peep sight that will mount on the Remington pump rifles. Bryce M. Towsley photo.

buck or to see better in poor light. They paint around the outside of the peep with red paint to help it stand out.

Shane shoots with the standard open sights, and Larry went back to open sights a few years ago. He said he wanted to give them a try again for awhile. He says that he may go back to the peep that served him so well for so many years, but states that he sees little reason for a scope on any rifle he hunts with. Of course, once again, most of the deer they

take are shot in the thick woods at close range and iron sights are fine.

Consider, though, that Larry has also hunted in Montana, Saskatchewan, and Newfoundland, where he has taken game with his iron-sighted rifles at distances that most of us scope users would have to think about.

(I should note that in 1997 I showed Larry a 7600 .35 Whelen rifle that I had mounted with a Leupold 1.75 - 5 Vari-X III scope, and to say the least I had his interest. Part of that is because, while they were

This is the author's Remington 7600 in .35 Whelen with a Leupold 1.5-5 Scope. While the Benoits favor peep sights many hunters like a low-power scope. Bryce M. Towsley photo.

all hitting the bullseye on a sight-in target I told them I was going to shoot the wood screw that was supporting it, and did. In all fairness, at 73 years old Larry's eyes are not what they used to be and iron sights are harder to see. Also, he really liked the small, compact size of the scope. I think that by next season he will be using one on his rifle. Is this the start of a trend? Only time will tell.)

It all boils down to skill and the willingness to practice until you achieve it. The Benoits have all put in that hard work because they know that chances at monster bucks are often fleeting and rarely repeated. They know that trophy bucks just don't make that many mistakes and you must be ready to capitalize on every one they do make. If you miss, that's your fault.

The Benoits practice with their rifles until they are ready for anything. For a "final exam" they like to throw a can of beans in the air and "explode" it with a rifle bullet.

After that, a buck's chest looks pretty big through those sights.

Chapter 11

Off the Norris Branch

One of the more controversial stories that have come out of Larry's long hunting career has been when he shot what was certainly the biggest buck of his life only to lose it to a winter storm. He set the record straight by telling the story in his book The Beginning—Where it All Began.

It is not only a great hunting tale, but one of survival against the elements and certainly one of tragedy. Here, in Larry's own words, is what really happened.

Larry Benoit. Benoit photo.

The storm that dropped 8 inches of snow during the night was tapering off. A west wind scattered the remaining snowflakes that dipped and curved in and out of the headlights. The air was slightly damp and I knew more snow was going to fall. We were 45 minutes outside of Moosehead Lake, on the Norris Branch, just off the Golden Road. The Norris Branch road led to nowhere except behind it lay a big swamp and, if you kept going in a straight line, Canada. I knew there was a big buck in that swamp.

Shane sat next to me as I weaved the Blazer around the potholes. It was the 21st of November, 1981. It was a time of silence as we both anticipated the hunt that the day would bring us. The country we were driving through was slightly rolling and thick with third growth spruce. There were clumps of balsam, cedar, and scrawny growths of hardwoods popping up on the hillsides. Small streams, lakes, and swamps intermingled around us for 20 miles in all directions. It was wild country, and in those days no camps were built within these woods. There were only the remains of long ago camps that had gone down with time. It wasn't an area you could drive into. The only people familiar with it were cat hunters. I knew that somewhere beyond the end of the Norris Brook road was one helluva animal.

Shane, my youngest son and closest hunting partner, and I felt in our blood that we were going to be on some big bucks that day. We planned to scout into the swamp and double team the big buck that we knew was in there. We spotted the track of a big buck that cut across the road in the fresh snow. Shane decided to follow him and disappeared into the woods in a northerly direction. I drove west a couple of miles and parked my Blazer.

The snow underfoot was soft and packed silently. It was a good tracking snow. Hardwoods lay next to the road, gently sloped up a hill then dipped into swamps of tangled, wind-whipped brush.

Shane and I had been hunting since the first day of the season in early November. At first, there had been no snow, but my sons had still done well.

Lane downed his biggest buck yet, it was a 248-pound 8-pointer, taken on the third day of the season. During the second week, Lanny took a 240 pounder on new snow just 15 minutes after he found his tracks.

I was in good shape. I was carrying a lot of excess weight in the spring, 198 pounds on my 5-foot 8-inch frame. During the summer, while doing sheet rock taping I dieted and exercised. Three weeks of walking every day through miles and miles of Maine woods, scouting, and tracking, knocked my weight down to 175 and built up my stamina. I felt loose, clearheaded, ready to travel and hunt.

I slipped into the woods and swung on a line north by northwest. It didn't take long to find the first tracks. They were in front of a mass of blowdowns. Two does following a medium-sized buck. I estimated him to be a 6-pointer from the signs I read in the snow. They were meandering and browsing as they moved through the cedars and blowdowns. My blood began to sing; I knew it was going to be a good day. Any experienced deer hunter will tell you the same: you can almost smell those days when the deer are moving and feeding, your senses are extra sharp.

The tracks headed northwest, and I followed them thinking that the does might attract a bigger buck. In 15 minutes, I caught up with them. The buck was a 6-pointer and the three deer browsed nonchalantly in front of me about 35 yards away. I didn't want to alert them so I left their tracks and moved to the northwest into the large swamp. It was here I hoped to find the buck, the one that had been through the week before—I had seen his tracks on and off.

It was light now and up through the treetops I saw a leaden sky, sullen with snow. I stopped to peel some birch bark from a tree, crumbled it up, and sifted it into a plastic pouch, which I stuck in the large pocket I have sewn into the back of my hunting shirt. I always do that if the weather looks bad, because the birch bark makes a quick-flaming tinder. If I don't use it, I throw it away at the end of the day.

About half an hour later, I came upon a set of tracks that cut through the swamp, heading west

into the coming storm. Those tracks set my heart to twitching as I glanced at their pattern, then I brushed the snow off to take a closer look. They were deeply staggered by one hefty swingbagger. The track was spread wide in the back and flat-tened from the weight it supported. All of the track was crisply and deeply imprinted into the ground. The snow was packed extra tight under the track, another sign that this deer was carrying a lot of weight. As I knelt down looking at the track, I said

Shane with a 218-pound, 10-point taken in 1981. Benoit photo.

to myself, "He's back and making his swing. It's an old swamp buck and he's about an hour and a half ahead of me."

That track kicked loose a squirt of adrenaline and I felt like a young kid again. That buck hadn't laid down yet. I noticed he wasn't feeding and was moving along briskly. He was looking for does that might have strayed into his territory. That buck had a 3-1/2-foot stride and had probably been going at that pace since daybreak. Although he had a 4 to 5-mile head start, I knew he would slow down to find a bed.

I followed that buck at a brisk pace, but not so fast that I would tire or stumble onto the buck in his bed. The depth of the snow made it extra quiet. The swamp hoosier led me over the hardest route he could find in this timber country. He sneaked under blowdowns and busted through the balsam and spruce as if he had a date up ahead, late, and horny as all get out. New snow hung on the trees. The smaller aspens and pin cherries were bent over from the weight. The spruces were black splotches against the whiteness of the snow.

I kept moving at a good clip. Snow covered my hat and shirt—I must have looked like a snowman. I carried my rifle slung upside down to keep the snow out of the barrel.

Now the deer was headed north by northeast. As he strode into a cluster of hardwoods that populated a small hill, the track became hesitant. I slowed down, unslung my rifle, and blew out the snow that clogged my peepsight. I moved into the stalk mode, creeping and pussyfooting along and eyeballing the terrain.

He had circled the hill and had laid down for a while. I came onto his tracks. The track was so fresh, the snow was crumbling into it. I knew that the buck had laid down on the hill to have a good view of his back track. After his snooze he got up, made a circle over his old track, which I saw, and headed on his quest.

That buck was mighty close to me. Then I got the feeling that something was looking at me. I turned my head very slowly to the right. I saw him standing there, 50 yards or so away. His head was up, motionless as if he were cut out of marble. For a brief moment, our eyes locked. As I raised my rifle, I thought how godawful big he was and how far into the swamp I was. He was so large, I had no trouble placing my peepsight behind his shoulder.

"God, he looks like a horse," I said to myself. I could have killed him then, but I didn't. Then, all hell broke loose. With electrifying power, the buck leaped down a sharp incline, spraying snow as his rear legs punched him into high gear. His antlers were walnut brown and his hair a dark, deep chestnut color. I saw his antlers and his drop tines. His neck, chest, and legs were what got me—they were huge, thick, and massive. "He's big, I can never drag him out of this swamp alone," I thought.

The buck whirled around and ran deeper into the white swamp. I was 5 hours into the swamp and I knew that I had 5 hours back out of the swamp.

"God almighty, he's the biggest buck that I've ever seen," I thought. I loped after the track. A few minutes later the buck materialized about 80 yards away, outlined against the snowy swamp. "I've got to have him," I said to myself as I leveled the front sight just back of the shoulder and squeezed the trigger.

Snowflakes big as half dollars fell. The wind had picked up slightly, warning that another storm from Canada was on its way. The heaviness of the snow in the air and hanging from the trees muffled the rifle shot so that it sounded like a popgun.

The buck humped and ran for 30 yards before he dropped. My bullet had exploded his lungs. A deer dies quickly when shot in the rib age, but he was still alive when I walked up to him. "Sorry old fellow," I murmured. It's always like this at the end, a sadness I feel when the hunt is over. The deer died looking up at me.

I looked at this monster deer, then I set to work. I cleaned him out, cleaned my knife and hands with the snow, and tore the tag from my license. I didn't have a pencil, so I signed it with the tip of a bullet. Then I folded the tag and tied it to the buck's

Larry Benoit has shot a lot of big bucks and has endured a lot of storms, but no buck was bigger or any storm more memorable than in 1981. Photo courtesy The Vermont Sportsman.

antler. Only then, with my work done, did I move back and admire the buck. He had 8 perfectly matched points with two drop tines 7 or 8 inches long. There were four or five nubs an inch or so long that circled the base. Using my rifle, I measured from the bottom of the shoulder to the high point of the back. The depth of the brisket was 23-1/2 inches. A buck weighing 175 to 200 pounds would measure between 18 and 19 inches. I grabbed an antler and tugged just to feel the heft of the deer. I could move it but I knew that I could never drag it alone. Once I dragged a 275-pound buck that I had shot. I could only move him 15 feet at a time. I don't know how big this buck was but it was bigger than any that I had shot before. It went at least 280 to 290 pounds.

I shot the buck at about 11:30 in the morning. The weather was turning worse than ever. The wind had picked up and the snow was blowing cutting down visibility. My first thought was to build a fire and prepare to spend the night. I had told Shane that if I didn't get out of the woods, I had my buck and the next morning we would bring him out together. I gathered some wood to make a fire next to my buck. I took out the birch bark and my matches. It was then I found that the plastic bag holding the matches had ruptured and the matches were useless. I also have a special pocket sewn into my hunting shirt to hold a Bic lighter. The night before, someone had needed a light for their suckweed and never returned my lighter.

Of all the years I have explained woods survival to my children and others, of all the stupid mistakes that anyone could make, I made them all. I sat there and looked at the dead matches, the pile of kindling, and my buck. I felt the snow coming down. Perhaps not having the matches made up my mind, but I decided to walk out of the woods and come back in the morning with Shane and Lanny and drag out the buck. I had done that many times before.

I rolled the deer into a blowdown and covered it with spruce boughs so the ravens wouldn't pick at him. I took a .270 cartridge, scraped my initials on

it with my knife and put it in the deer's rectum. I took one last admiring look at the buck and pointed myself towards the road.

The snow had really started to come down by now. It was blowing out of Canada and up to my knees. My green wool shirt was powdered white and I could feel the snow dribble down my back. As I set out, I tore my three red handkerchiefs into strips and tied them on saplings on my way out. I started backtracking towards the road. It had taken 5 hours to get in. I figured that I could get out in 4. Pretty soon, the tracks that I had made in the morning were covered and I let my instinct lead me.

By 4:00 it was too dark to see. The going had been a lot tougher than I had expected. I heard Shane shoot one shot, which was our signal but the falling snow made it impossible to be sure from where the shot had come. All I know it that I heard it. Did it come from my left or my right? Did it come from my rear? I had no idea. All that I was sure of was that behind me was a mammoth buck that I had shot in the white swamp.

It was turning black and I couldn't see 10 feet. I had a small green flashlight. I turned it on. About 2 hours later, the light began to flicker and dim. I knew the light wasn't going to last me to the road. The light that I use is guaranteed to last 48 hours. Maybe mine was bad or the cold drew down the batteries.

The snow was as high as my kneecaps. Blowdowns were all around me. With the darkness, I could stumble and fall or gouge out an eye with a stick poking through the snow, as lethal as lances.

Shane fired again and I answered. He wasn't far I knew but I wasn't going to walk through these woods in the dark. I had light enough to make my way to a stand of balsam that would act as a wind break. I knocked the snow off the branches. I reached into my shirt and pulled out a peanut butter and jelly sandwich, which I ate.

"Dummy," I kept muttering to myself. No matches, no flashlight. It was going to be a cold night. I was getting mad at myself. I was safe with my back against the sturdy balsams. I pulled my

Some bucks in front of the Benoit's house. Year after year they load the game pole to the breaking point. Benoit photo.

wool shirt over my head and zipped it up so my breath would be trapped inside. It would help me stay warm. I remained standing, leaning against the trees. I knew better than to lie down. I felt that everything was in my favor. I wasn't cold or worried about freezing to death even though I had no fire. I was not completely exhausted so it was not a question that I had to sleep or stay awake to survive the night. I knew that if I was so exhausted that I would die if I went to sleep, I sure wouldn't have gone to sleep.

Being alone in the woods during a storm is an experience that's hard to explain to the common layman. I know that two people lost in the woods often have less of a chance of survival. Would I have dared to say, or even suggest to a buddy that we may not survive the night? I know that if doubt gets into the minds of two people together, one can almost convince the other that death is climbing down the tree toward you.

But, if you are alone, you can look at yourself and say, "You stupid, dumb S.O.B., how can you be so stupid dumb, anyway? After braying and harping about woods safety for so many years, you dummy made all the mistakes." Once you make those mistakes, the woods are right there to correct you mighty quick. You make yourself mad and sometimes that madness can be the essence of survival.

I dozed leaning against the tree. When I began to crumble, I would wake up and exercise my feet and arms. I had on a T-shirt, a light flannel, my wool hunting shirt, light underwear, and my wool hunting pants. I was warm enough leaning against the tree. Fifteen minutes lying down and hypothermia could lead me to death.

At midnight, the wind was fierce as it roared through the tree tops. Branches snapped and trees crashed. About 2:00 a.m., the wind died and the temperature dropped. I estimated that it was in the low teens. Ice coated on the outside of my jacket. About this time, Shane fired again at spaced intervals. The shots clipped the trees overhead, he was close. I shot back and waited for first light.

The woods lightened from black to gray. The first thing I did was backtrack a mile towards my buck. My tracks from the day before were covered with snow as if I had never been there. I turned back to my campsite. Now it was light enough, and I looked up and saw the outline of the logging road. I was exactly 50 yards from it when I settled against the balsams in the darkness for the night. With the driving snow, the blowdowns, and the branches, it might as well have been 2 miles.

About a half an hour later I was walking down the logging road when the game warden, Gary Sargent came up on his snow machine. "You Larry Benoit?" he asked. "Yep," I answered. "We've been looking for you. You been lost?" "Haven't been lost, nope. I knew where I was all night, my light failed," I replied.

I found Shane, and after a good breakfast, we went looking for my buck. The swamp was like a sea where a ship had gone down. Nothing was visible except snow. Snow covered the ground, the trees, and the branches. All of the landmarks of the day before were buried under white, bleached on white. We searched all day zigzagging north by northeast. The next day, I went back with Lanny and crisscrossed the swamp. It was as if the deer had never existed. It was like this hunt had been a dream and the day in the white swamp had been an illusion.

In hunts gone by I had left deer that I had shot in the woods when it became too late to drag them. But always, I left them on mountains with landmarks and a track to follow. A swamp after a blizzard—it looks all the same. It's hard to describe unless you have been there, unless you've hunted in one of those big swamps. You don't just walk right back and pinpoint your deer. It's not like sticking your thumb on a map and saying this is where I was. That thumb can cover 20 square miles.

"I knew I shouldn't have shot," I told Lanny. I have thought of what I had done a hundred times since. I should have never left the buck, I should have stayed there until morning. Then I would have had a fresh back track to follow when it was

clear light. I probably got a little upset when I found that I had no matches. I figured I could get out of the woods in easy time. I didn't count on the blizzard in the swamp.

Swamps, I hate swamps! I hunt them because up in Maine, that's where the big bucks hide. If I had my druthers, I would prefer to hunt them after they leave the swamps and start to make their swing on the side of a mountain. Hunters have asked me a lot of questions about that day. "Why didn't I blaze a trail?"

If I had blazed a trail, it would have taken me 12 hours instead of 5 to get to the stand of trees where I spent the night. I also know that you can't make much of a mark on a frozen tree with a hunting knife. Why don't I carry a hatchet or a roll of fluorescent tape? If I carried every thing that has been suggested, I would never be able to catch up with the deer in the first place.

When I knew deep inside that I had lost that buck, we headed home to Vermont. Shane had shot a 218 pound, 11-pointer the day Lanny and I searched for my buck. Nowadays, more people hunt this swamp. Somewhere in there is a loaded .270 cartridge with the initials L.E.B. etched onto the case. That will be all that is left of the biggest buck of my life.

Chapter 12

Tips, Techniques, and Tactics

"The hardest part is finding a big buck. The easiest part is getting 'em out."

-Larry Benoit

Double Teaming

Before he left us, well before his time, Jerry Cassel was married to my father's younger sister. He had a unique view on life, never taking it too seriously, but always thinking about the way it all worked. He was a great outdoor companion, and he and I spent a lot of time hunting or fishing together, during which he used to like to speculate on the ways of things. When you spend that much time talking with somebody the conversation is liable to take some interesting turns. I vividly remember one time when he said, "Assume for a moment that deer can think and reason like we can. Then try to imagine if you were a big, trophy buck and you knew you had a Benoit on your trail.

You know you are in big trouble and there's not much you can do to avoid it. Can you think of anything worse?"

Actually, I can...two Benoits on my trail.

They love to double team when tracking big bucks, and that undoubtedly is a trophy whitetail's darkest nightmare.

The idea is that two sets of eyes will see a deer faster, two sets of ears will hear him better, and two brains will out-think him quicker than one.

One year Shane and Larry double teamed for three big bucks in a six-day period, including a day lost to traveling. The first one was a 200-pound 9-point that Shane shot in Maine on Saturday. With their Maine tags filled they used Sunday to head home to Vermont and a couple of days later they

Larry (left) and Shane in 1985. The bucks were double teamed. Benoit photo.

double teamed another 9-point buck for Larry, which dressed out at 220 pounds. Then they teamed up on a 210-pound 8-point for Shane on Thanksgiving day. Three trophy bucks, all over 200 pounds, all taken by double teaming.

Larry says, "You have to see a buck before you can shoot him and they always seem to be in the toughest place to do that. It's a simple fact that two sets of eyes are better than one. With two hunters, you double the chances of seeing that buck. Actually you more than double them because one hunter can watch the track while the other hunter can concentrate exclusively on looking for the buck. This is better than one hunter who has to watch both the track and for the deer.

Double teaming takes a couple of hunters who work well together. They must learn to anticipate each other's moves and learn to think like one another. You can't spend a lot of time in discussion when you are close to a trophy buck, so they both should be experienced trackers with similar styles who can get on with the job at hand. It also helps to have somebody with a similar stride length and, due to the difficulties of this style of hunting, it is important to have a partner that you are comfortable with and can trust, one who stays cool in fast breaking situations.

"The way we work it," says Shane, "is the front guy will follow the track while the back guy walks in his tracks and looks for the deer. He doesn't worry about the track, he leaves that up to the lead hunter. Instead the rear hunter just keeps looking for the deer. He will place his feet in the same tracks that the lead hunter is making. This insures that he has a clean, quiet place to step without having to look or think about it. Because the first hunter has already stepped there he knows that it is a safe place to put his feet without sticks to break or trip him up. We try to walk in unison so that our movements are coordinated and we take the same

Larry with a 220-pound, 9-point Vermont buck he and Shane double teamed in 1985. Benoit photo.

steps at the same time. This cuts down on the noticeable movements. All our movements are fluid and slow and they all have a reason. We don't make any motions that aren't completely necessary, we don't wave our hands around or make any unnecessary movements to alert the buck. That means no waving around handkerchiefs, taking your hat on and off, or any other unnecessary movements. Don't pull yourself up the hills by grabbing trees. This causes the tree to move and alerts deer that can't see you, but can see the taller tree. Also, the hand movement is a giveaway. The deer can see all these things from a long way off and will be gone before you know he is there. A fluid, methodical movement is more natural to the woods. It looks more like the way a deer, moose, or bear moves. The deer are used to seeing this type of movement and they will let you get away with more than you can with fast or unnatural movements. That doesn't mean they won't see you and

run off, it's just that they seem to take longer to notice and react to this kind of movement. It is important to be quiet, of course. You must be careful where you are placing your feet, just as you would any other time you are hunting. All this takes a little practice, but it is easier than you might think once you have a team that works well together."

Because each hunter has a little different perspective on the woods, each can see a little differently and so either one can potentially spot the buck first. However, it is usually the rear hunter who sees him. That's simply a matter of the odds. The rear hunter is looking more and is not worried about following the track, and the odds are that he will be more likely to see the buck.

Sometimes just a few feet can make a big difference in whether or not you can see the deer. Just being a little left or right, or sometimes even if you are a little taller or shorter, can make an amazing difference. It can open up a hole in the brush that isn't

Lanny (left) and Landon with a 228-pound buck they double teamed in 1989. Benoit photo.

visible from another angle, and one hunter might see a buck that the other hunter cannot see.

If the lead hunter suddenly stops and steps to the side, that is the signal for the rear hunter to step to the other side. It is important to understand this because of safety. When things are happening fast you want somebody behind you that you can trust to be safe and the back hunter wants somebody in front who will do what is expected and not step in the way. Whoever sees the buck first will hiss, speak softly, or touch the other hunter as a signal to freeze or step to the side.

"We always stay together," say Larry. "A big buck can cover a lot of ground and if you are splitting up and trying to circle on him you will just be wasting time. You can't know for sure where the buck is heading. Those big bucks have a lot of tricks up their sleeves and many times you will guess wrong. Then you wind up losing time and making unnecessary noise and commotion trying to get back together. It's better to stay together and to go where the track goes. This is true even when you are sure you are close to the buck. That's when the extra eyes are most important, and if you split up you won't know what the other guy is doing. Lots of times, too, the buck isn't bedded where you thought he would be, and again hunters who split up will just lose more time trying to find each other. If you stay together things just work better."

Another advantage to double teaming is that you can stay with the buck longer. If you are alone you might have to leave the track in mid-afternoon to get back to your truck by dark. But, if you can send one hunter back for the truck to drive it to the closest road (it helps to know your country) the other can stay with the track a little longer. Also,

Shane Benoit takes a break from dragging. Benoit photo.

anybody who has ever dragged a 200-pound buck out of the woods knows the obvious advantage of two hunters together. It is hard work to skid out a big buck, and if you happen to have your favorite hunting partner along to share the burden it goes much easier.

Backtracking

"One time we came on some fresh tracks of a doe, a couple of fawns, and a small buck," Larry said. "I suspect that most hunters would not have even looked twice at them, but I told Shane that I thought that the way the buck was hounding and pestering her, the doe was getting ready to come into heat. He was following her close and smelling her tracks often and generally making a pest of himself. He was probably a 2-1/2 year old buck and would have dressed about 160 pounds or so; some hunters would have liked to shoot him, but he wasn't anything we wanted. That little buck may have thought he was going to get lucky, but I knew that there was at least one good buck up on that mountain where they just came from. Sooner or later he was going to cross the doe's tracks and when he did he would follow her. By the time she was ready to breed, the little guy would have been run off. That is, unless we helped him out and spoiled the big fella's plans. I figured that if we followed her tracks back the way she came we

Shane with a 210-pound, 8-point Vermont buck he and Larry backed-tracked in 1985. This buck has a 22-inch inside spread. Benoit photo.

would run into him sooner or later. While he would be preoccupied with the idea of a doe in heat up ahead, he wouldn't be stupid, so we had to be careful. Because of his direction of travel he would be facing right at us so we would have to be sure that he didn't see us first. We had the element of surprise, we knew he would be on the trail, but he didn't have a clue we were around and looking for him.

"We started backtracking that doe and it wasn't long before I told Shane, 'There's your buck. Hurry up and shoot him, he won't hang around all day!' That 8-point dressed out at 210 pounds. Shane shot him at about 30 yards. It was like he ran up to us and posed saying 'Here I am guys, shoot me.'

"Backtracking a hot doe is a great way to find a big buck. My dad taught me how to do it years and years ago and I have done it a lot of times and taken

A 210-pound, 8-point Vermont buck lies where he fell after Shane and Larry backed-tracked him in 1985. Benoit photo.

a lot of good bucks that way. I suppose you could just wait for the buck on the trail, but this makes it happen a lot faster."

Listen to the Woods

True hunters are predators and predators are in tune with the woods.

Trackers, to be successful, must be true hunters.

Trackers are human predators, perhaps the ultimate predators because they have the ability to think and to reason. While other deer hunters can enjoy the success of killing deer and even trophy bucks, without ever learning the woods, trackers cannot—they must become part of their environment or they will never truly see success.

They listen to the sounds and detect subtle changes. They recognize that when a red squirrel is scolding up ahead or the blue jays are screaming on the side of the mountain there is a reason. They know, too, that there is a reason for silence. To be successful you must learn to listen to the woods. Know that the ravens have flushed from the beaver pond ahead because of something that has happened there. Perhaps the buck you are tracking has spooked them, or maybe it was a coyote. But, what caused the coyote to leave his daytime bed and move? Could it have been a doe? If so, what is she running from? Is another hunter ahead or is she coming close to estrus and is tired of bucks harassing her? Did she see your buck and run? Is there another buck? Will your buck move into the open and allow a shot or has he turned and headed into the deep swamp? Should you pause and wait a moment or continue?

Is the reason that the jays or squirrels are yelling because of the passage of the buck you are tracking? Why did they suddenly stop and become quiet? We can't tell you in a book, because every situation is different. You must evaluate each one

Larry likes to leave his initials where he has taken a buck. Benoit photo.

on its own. What we can do is make you think about it.

If you watch the woods around you they will tell you a story. See the birds that suddenly fly off, the grouse that flushes, or the rabbit that runs from cover and it will tell you a lot.

Shuck your civilized oblivity to your surroundings and tune in to the woods. Be alert to what is happening and know that it rarely happens without a reason. Then learn to interpret what that reason may be. Only then will you start to become an efficient predator.

Shane Benoit on the trail of a good buck. Bryce M. Towsley photo.

Tracking Wounded Deer

Big, trophy bucks are different from other deer in a lot of ways, not the least of which is a tenacity to life that isn't mirrored in other segments of the whitetail's society. These big bucks are the best of the best. Nature's selection process has made them the biggest, the strongest, and the proudest. That last characteristic may well be the determining factor. They are proud of their dominance, a dominance that they earned on the battle field. They have learned not to give up, to keep going, to fight to the end. If he is the dominant buck in the area, he became so by fighting all challengers. Only a buck with the will to continue can win.

This can make them hard to kill. Certainly a well-placed bullet through both lungs, the heart, spine, or brain will put any deer down for good, but the marginal hits will write a different story. When other deer will often give up and die, these big, tough bucks keep going.

A good tracker with snow will likely still get the buck, unless the hit is superficial. If his track was able to be followed before, then certainly now it will be even easier. Blood, or a different gait due to injuries, will make his trail even easier to follow. Shock, weakness, and confusion from his wounds will have him making mistakes that he would not have made, and barring unforeseen problems, the outcome has already been determined. If it is on bare-ground and the deer is not leaving much of a blood trail the outcome can go either way. It can turn into a long and frustrating day. However, the hunter can make it safer, faster, and easier by paying attention to certain details.

First, know that even with the shot going exactly where you wanted it to, things can happen. Lanny once shot a 268-pound buck in the neck with his .270 Winchester and he hurt him bad, even damaging some vertebrae. He moved on the trail, thinking that the deer must be dead and jumped him from his first bed. That deer ran a long way—miles and miles—before he was able to finally take him. If he had been able to shoot

him in the bed the first time he caught up with him it would have been a lot easier.

When a deer is hit, initially it will be in shock. A modern rifle bullet hits hard and transfers a lot of energy. The buck will be dazed and confused for a little while. He may run off on instinct, the survival reaction, but his brain isn't usually working with all segments firing.

There is also a phenomenon called "neural shock" that can cause a deer to react to a non-fatal shot. This has been documented by Swedish researchers and detailed in an article in a 1988 issue of the *Journal of Trauma*. In the test, pigs were moderately anesthetized to eliminate pain as a reactive factor. Monitoring their brain wave functions, the researchers then shot them in the back legs, a nonlethal area. The pigs showed a clear and immediate suppression of brain activity, some lasting for 30 seconds or more. This was not a result of a loss of blood pressure, but strictly from shock. In two-

thirds of the pigs, there was also respiratory arrest for up to 45 seconds, which further indicates shock acting on and suppressing the brain waves. This is likely one of the primary reasons that deer sometimes go down like they are dead, only to recover and run off.

Regardless of if a deer runs off at the hit or drops, you should react quickly and correctly. Always put another round in the chamber of your rifle as fast as you can. If he is running off, try to shoot him again. No matter how well you think you have him hit, if he is on his feet and you have an opportunity to shoot again, shoot! Don't stand and admire your shot—"dead" deer have a way of running off, never to be found. More than once I have had hunters argue with me about this, "I shot him right in the heart, how far can he go?" More than once we have found out. Don't worry about ruining meat; how much will be ruined if he escapes? And don't worry about ruining the cape. My friend Pete Lajoie is

Lanny caught this 240-pound buck in his bed in 1980. Benoit photo.

one of the top whitetail taxidermists in the country and he has shown me that they can work miracles on a damaged cape. I saw one buck that was hit with an arrow that protruded from his shoulder and into his neck. Every time the buck moved it cut more of his neck hide. By the time the hunter recovered the deer it looked like he had attacked it with a dull chain saw. Today that deer is on the hunter's living room wall and it looks pretty good. The worst case is if you have to buy another cape and,

compared to the cost in heartbreak and guilt from a lost trophy, they are cheap. Keep shooting! Even if he is down, but has his head up, keep shooting.

If the deer simply drops, keep the sights on his chest for several seconds or perhaps a minute. If nothing happens, put on your safety and go make your peace with your buck, but watch him and be ready to shoot. Approach from behind and stay clear of his rack and his hooves; both can hurt you badly so fast you won't believe it. If his eyes are

Approach a downed buck with caution and be ready to shoot again if necessary. Bryce M. Towsley photo.

shut, he is alive, so shoot again. If they are open, reach out and touch one with your rifle barrel, and if he blinks he is still alive.

If he runs off, go to where he was when you first shot, but take your time, the deer may still be close and in shock. They can recover quickly, particularly if you jump them up. Look for indications of a hit, blood, or hair. Try to recognize the hair and identify where it came from. The same with the blood, but that is harder. The one exception may be lung blood, but if you hit his lungs it doesn't matter, he isn't going far. Look at the hair and try to visualize where on the buck it came from. Recently I was asked to evaluate some deer hair from a Texas buck. Everybody there had a different idea of where it came from, but mine was unique. I said I thought it was the white hair from low on a deer's butt. There was a camera crew filming a television show and later we watched the footage to see the hunter's bullet graze the inside of the buck's rear leg. He had learned a lesson, but was not seriously hurt.

A lot of hair usually indicates a grazing shot and is not a good sign. Bone chips are almost always from a leg hit—also bad. Look on the ground behind where the deer was standing. Is there blood or lung tissue? Are there any stomach contents to indicate a gut shot?

Try to remember how the buck reacted to the shot. Did he lurch or buck? A heart shot buck will often "mule kick" before running off. How did he run off? Did he look fine, or was he "running funny" or hunched up? A hunched up buck is usually gut shot.

Did you hear the bullet hit the deer? Someone who is listening for the sound will almost always hear the bullet when it strikes home. That is an excellent indication of a hit, and the sound can give you some clues to the location. A loud crack can be a leg hit in the bone. A solid wet thump, usually described as the sound hitting a watermelon might make, indicates either a good lung shot or a gut shot. A heavier thump might mean shoulders or other solid meaty areas backed up with bone.

If you need to track the buck, first mark where he and you were at the shot for later reference. You may need to come back and start over, and it can be surprisingly hard to find these places. Use a paper towel or toilet paper rather than plastic surveying tape because these will disintegrate in a few days if you don't come back.

If you are lucky you will find the buck in the first 200 yards or less. If you don't, the hit was probably not one that will be quickly fatal. A wounded buck can run a long way in a very short time. He may die within a few minutes, a few hours, or not at all. You have no way of knowing so you must assume the worse—that he is still alive—and act accordingly.

Stay calm and resist the temptation to rush ahead. I failed to follow that advice one time and jumped the buck from his first bed. Once that happens it can be tough, because they get a shot of endorphins and adrenaline and they seem to get supercharged. It turned out I had broken his leg and I tracked that buck for nearly 10 miles. I waded across a waist deep stream three times in 15 degree weather, and it took me two days to get him. If I had slowed down I might have ended it in a few minutes.

Shane advises that, "A wounded buck will run off, but as soon as he feels safe he will lie down in first thick cover he comes to. It is important to 'death creep' him right from the start. Once they get past shock and you jump them, they can keep going. Be even more careful than you would be on a bedded, unwounded buck. This one knows you are after him and he will be watching. Make your first approach on him the best you are capable of and try to shoot him again in his bed. Look ahead to see the blood trail and watch where it is going. Even though you are excited, try hard to slow down and sneak on him."

Remember this is now a wounded buck, so any bullet you can put in him is a bonus. Take any shot you have—you can't make it any worse. Stay with him no matter what. If you are able to continue on his trail you must. You have an obligation to the deer for nothing less.

Listen to the Deer

Even after you kill him a buck can tell you a lot about what is happening where he lived. Look at his feet. Are they chipped and worn or are they smooth and in good shape? A mountain buck will likely have feet that are showing the ravages of walking on bedrock and the loose rocks exposed by the thin soil conditions of the mountain tops. A buck that lives his life in the swamps has better looking feet. The soft, boggy conditions make easier walking that does less damage to them. The feet of a swamp buck may have some chips that are new and fresh. Usually these are a result of his travels in search of friendly does. A buck that has the well-pedicured feet of a swamp buck, but with damage that still has sharp edges, has been wandering. That would indicate that the rut is beginning or is in full swing.

Look at the buck for fresh cuts, scrapes, broken antler tines, torn ears, or patches of missing hair. If he shows indications of fighting you know that there is another buck of similar size and social status living near to him. This might be a good place for those in your party with unfilled tags to keep hunting. If he has tine marks in his butt, put there as he ran from defeat, that would indicate that the other buck is bigger and that would be a great place to hunt.

Check his stomach contents. What has he been eating? Does some of it look older than the rest? If so, and you can identify what the food is, then you may be able to reconstruct where he has traveled in the past few hours.

All of this might not be of any use to you if you have filled your tag, but it can be very helpful to your hunting partners. If the buck is somebody else's, you can use the clues to help you find one of your own to shoot.

Getting Them Out

Larry has a saying that he is very fond of—it goes like this:

"The hardest part is finding a big buck.
The easiest part is getting 'em out."

That might well be true, but it doesn't change the fact that getting them out is tough! It is certainly a lot less fun than finding and hunting a big buck. But, for most hunters it is all part of the package. For most of us, without total involvement in the hunt it is somehow diminished. Part of that total involvement is in "getting 'em out."

There isn't any magic way to get a buck out of the woods. Like Larry said when I asked, "Tie your rope around his horns and take a half-hitch on his nose. Tie the other end to a stick, point your nose at the road, and pull."

The best advice is not to be in any hurry. Your hunt is over and you have the rest of the season to get this buck out of the woods. Calm down and think a little. You might remember a road or trail that is closer. Think your route through before you start dragging. If you have a map, get it out and figure out where you are and where you have to go. If you know the area use your memory. Try to anticipate any obstacles such as a brook, river, lake, ravine, cliff, or swamp. Plan how you will avoid them, because it is hard enough dragging a 250-pound buck without adding to the problems. If the snow peters out as you drop in elevation try to stay as high as you can for as long as you can. A buck will drag much harder on bare-ground than it will on snow, so try to keep him on the white stuff as long as possible. Also, try to stay high as long as you can to have gravity work for you. If you drop down too early or in the wrong place it is a lot tougher to drag a buck uphill than it is downhill. Be careful on the steep downhill sections that the buck doesn't start sliding and run over you. The antlers of a buck can inflict serious stab wounds on your legs. The buck running over you can cause you to fall and slide yourself—the result can be a broken bone or worse.

Consider using a boat or canoe to get the buck out. If you can get it to an accessible lake or somewhere downriver this can save a lot of dragging.

Dave Coker tells about the time that Lanny shot a big buck way back in, so far and with terrain so thick that dragging that buck out would have been tough.

"We knew he was close to a river so Lanny, Shane, and I took a 12-foot aluminum boat with a

little four horsepower motor and we went exploring down a branch that met the river. There were two or three beaver dams that we had to cross and the whole thing turned into an adventure.

"After a while we came to a bigger river, but nothing looked familiar. We kept going until we hit some rapids. Lanny and Shane got out and waded through them and I took the boat and 'shot' the rapids. Then they all got back in and we went until we got to a waterfall. Lanny recognized the falls because he had tracked the deer by them and realized that we had gone too far, that the buck was behind us. He left on foot to look for the deer while Shane and I dragged the boat back by hand to get it back

up through the shallow rapids so we could use the motor again. Once we were back up past the rapids we found Lanny with a buck that weighed 247 pounds. He had left the deer by a little brook that was a tributary to the river and we had been looking for that, but the brook had gone underground and we missed it. At one point we had stopped and a raven went over. I said that raven is calling us to the deer, but we ignored it. It turns out that I was right and the deer was there.

"So there we were three men, all well over 200 pounds, this deer, and all our gear in this little boat. It was close to sinking so we had to leave the deer. Lanny and I went back in the next morning. The

Shane on the end of a drag rope. Benoit photo.

Lane with a buck that he dragged to the backside of a lake and later retrieved with a boat. Benoit photo.

Lanny Benoit and Dave Coker using a boat to retrieve Lanny's buck. Lanny took the 247-pound buck in 1995. Benoit photo.

river had frozen during the night and we had to break the ice to get through, but we made it and got the deer out. If we had tried dragging him out I think it would have taken forever."

Larry uses a stick of about 1-1/2 inches in diameter and 30 inches long. This length is good for one person or two to pull on. Using his knife, he cuts them from a live sapling and cuts a groove around the center to keep the rope from sliding off. The green wood is springy, tough, strong, and almost impossible to break. A dead stick picked up off the forest floor has a nasty habit of breaking at the most inopportune time, usually dumping you on your face in the mud.

Larry saves the sticks as souvenirs. Each one is unique in its own way, connected forever to a fallen monarch of the woods and to the Benoits who will immortalize his memory. There are dozens of these sticks at the camp and uncounted numbers at his house. Some of them are worn slick from the hands that pulled them for miles and miles and I only wish they could talk, because every one can tell a story.

Larry shows that even at 73 years old he can still "pull 'em out." Benoit photo.

*C*hapter 13

This and That

This chapter is a compilation of thoughts and ideas that each would not stand alone as a full chapter. That makes them no less important and there is much to be gained from reading what is here.

Larry Benoit with an 11-point, 222-pound Maine buck (1974). Photo courtesy The Vermont Sportsman.

Dealing with Fame

Amerrica in the late twentieth century has become in many ways a bitter place.

In the 1980s the most hated and targeted man in the country seemed to be Donald Trump, and now in the 1990s it is Bill Gates. Their only crime has been success. Americans love to beat up on the people who are winning. Instead of applauding success from hard work and talent, we ridicule it. Too many have learned that the top can indeed be a lonely place. I suppose the psychological explanation is that by criticizing and degrading the winners the losers boost their own power and credibility within their own minds.

The Benoits have hardly been exempt from all of this. For years and years they have been called poachers and worse. Critics are plentiful, and you will run into them every place that hunters gather. Usually some guy will claim to have "proof" that the Benoits shoot all of their deer at night. When asked to produce that proof he will claim that a friend of his brother-in-law's cousin saw it happen. I'll ask for the guy's name and telephone number and that's when the conversation will usually turn hostile.

Larry Benoit with Vermont bucks from 1972. Photo courtesy The Vermont Sportsman.

Even the long arm of the law will get in on the act. For a long time Lane had the same Maine Game Warden stopping his vehicle and checking his license almost daily. I suppose he figured that it would be a great coup to nab a high profile hunter and would get him more mileage with his boss than simply doing his job well. Regardless of the reason it bordered on harassment.

When I asked the Benoits about all of this they said it was even worse than what I thought, but that they simply try to ignore it for the most part.

"What can you do?" answered Shane. "It comes with the territory. We don't have to prove a thing to anybody, we only need to satisfy ourselves. We simply ignore it, we know that the vast majority of deer hunters out there are good, solid sportsmen who, like us, will work hard and enjoy a trophy only if they truly earned it. Why let a few jerks give them all a black mark?"

I don't suppose any of the Benoits are angels, but who among us is? I can, however, truthfully say that not only did I see nothing but exemplary be-

Left to right: Lanny, Shane, Lane, Landon, and Larry Benoit (1991). Benoit photo. Photo courtesy The Vermont Sportsman.

Larry (left) and Lanny Benoit in 1974. Photo courtesy The Vermont Sportsman.

havior when it came to Fish and Game laws during my associations with them, but at times I thought they were too cautious. If there was any question about the law, the law got the benefit of the doubt.

I would have to believe that shooting the numbers of big trophy bucks that the Benoits have taken over the years by using a light at night, in Northern Maine, would be a more difficult feat than would tracking them down and shooting them legitimately. Anybody who knows deer and knows the area would have to reach the same conclusion. In fact, I dare say it would be impossible. Furthermore, I have come to know the Benoits too well, and have come to understand their deep respect for whitetail deer and for deer hunting to ever believe that they would consider poaching a deer.

An illustration of how deep that respect for the whitetail goes was shown to me while working on the photos for this book. I was passing some pointers on to Shane and Larry on photography.

"When the tongue is hanging out of the deer's mouth, it spoils the photo," I said. "Take your knife and cut it off."

"I won't do it," replied Larry. "They are too majestic an animal to mutilate like that even in death. They deserve more respect. I'll just tuck it back inside his mouth."

Do you really believe a guy like that would shoot a buck at night, with a light, and then claim he tracked it down?

Nutrition

Hunting hard and walking all those miles will use up a lot of energy. It takes food to replace it, and if you plan to last the season, the right food is important. Tracking is hard work and it takes a toll on your body. You don't have the option of a "training schedule" when you only have a limited amount of time to kill a trophy buck. You have to hunt every day and all day if you hope to have any chance at success. Nutrition is important not only to maintaining the energy to keep going, but also to making sure that the body is as able as the mind is willing.

"When an athlete is training for a big endurance race he will load up on carbohydrates," Lanny told me. "But that doesn't necessarily work for tracking deer. Over the years I have paid a lot of attention to how I feel and what I eat and I think that we hunters have different requirements.

"Certainly you need the carbohydrates to maintain long-term energy and endurance. I'll eat a lot of pasta for that. I like spaghetti for supper with bread. Also during the day I eat a lot of canned spaghetti or Beef-a-Roni. This helps to maintain long-term energy and it's a lot better than candy. With that the sugar burns off too fast; carbohydrates will stay with you. That's not to say that sugar doesn't have its place. Sometimes when you are hunting and you are just done in, a candy bar will give you the boost you need to make it back to the truck. It's just that it is a temporary boost, you also need to concentrate on long term, all day energy.

"The difference is that an athlete in training will work hard for a day or two and then take a day off for his muscles to recover and repair themselves. He may work another part of his body while that part is healing or he may just rest. When we are deer hunting we can't do that, we need to keep going every day. We use our legs every day we hunt and our muscles get sore. That pain and lameness means that the muscles are damaged, but we can't sit around for a day or two and let them mend.

"Most hunters enter the deer season a little out shape, we work at our jobs all year and don't spend a lot of time tramping around in the woods. Even if we walk or jog, hunting those mountains and swamps uses a different set of muscles. When you go out the first day and get on a track and follow it for 8 or 10 miles you are going to feel it the next day. But, if you want to take a trophy buck you will have to get back out there hunting no matter what. You may want to stay in camp, but that won't fill any deer tags. This relentless pushing never really gives your muscles a chance to heal and mend before you are out there using them again.

"I think that you must have a good bit of protein in your diet as well as carbohydrates to give those muscles something to build up and mend with. Also, in that cold weather I think some fat in your diet is important, I really believe that it helps to keep you warmer. So, I will eat differently when I am off at hunting camp than I will when I am at home the rest of the year. I eat lots of bacon and eggs for breakfast for the protein and for the fat. I think that all the exercise of walking will offset the bad effects of the extra fat. I have found that with a high-protein breakfast and lots of carbohydrates during lunch and dinner, as well as some protein then too, I can keep hunting all day and day after day. I just seem to feel better when I eat this way and am hunting hard. My legs toughen up faster and don't stay as sore and lame for nearly as long. After a week or ten days of this I start to feel pretty good. I find that I can go all day. My legs and my wind are in good shape and I start to really feel like a deer hunter."

Survival

If you are going to be a tracker you will need to be able to penetrate deep into the wilderness with complete comfort and knowledge that your abilities will keep you safe. That doesn't mean, of course, that you should go unprepared. While the goal is always to leave the woods each day, things can happen that may cause you to spend a night. Weather can change fast, you can misjudge how far you are in, or you can even get lost. If you are tracking that means you will be dressed lightly and the most important aspect of your survival will be staying warm and getting dry. Never enter the woods without at least two ways to make a fire and make sure that both are waterproof.

Note that Larry made that mistake back at Norris Branch (Chapter 11) and it could have cost him dearly. He had loaned his lighter to a guy who didn't return it and his matches were wet. He had no fire, he had to spend the night in the woods, and there was a nor'easter storm raging—a less experienced man might not have lived. Larry had a couple of things going for him, one of which was his inherent toughness. He can take a lot more cold than many of us. The other was that he is completely comfortable in the woods, even at night in a storm. He simply found the best shelter he could, made do with what he had, and rode it out.

A disposable lighter should be one of the fire starting tools you have with you. Like so many other products in the country today, these have been

Never go into the woods without at least two ways to start a fire. Shown at left is a disposable butane lighter, the center is a candle designed for a backpacker's lantern which can aid in lighting damp tinder, and right is a magnesium fire starter. Bryce M. Towsley photo.

redesigned—made more idiot-proof—making it important that you check them out to find the right one. Most of the lighters today will have a non-adjustable flame and that flame will be low. These are useless for the outdoorsman. Look for a lighter that will make the biggest flame you can find. To start a fire with wet tinder, you will need it. If it doesn't have the childproof lock on it, so much the better, because these are a nuisance at best and with cold fingers they can be dangerous. They hardly work anyway; my son could figure them out from the time he was 4 years old. Because lighters can fail when they are wet, keep it in a dry place and don't use it until you need it for survival. Don't use it to light the lantern or stove at camp, don't use it for smoking, and never loan it out. It is better to keep a second lighter for all of that.

Waterproof matches are fairly good, but they deteriorate with age and while you carry them. Don't depend on them, but if you wish to keep them as a backup that's not a bad idea. The magnesium fire starters that most camping supply stores carry are excellent fire starters. They are completely waterproof and burn very hot to help ignite damp tinder. Forget looking glasses or anything like that, because the sun rarely shines in the North country in November, and besides, by the time you need a fire it will be getting dark.

A couple of small candles, such as those sold for hiking lanterns, will burn for a long time. If you light one and slide it under your tinder pile it will burn long enough to dry out damp tinder and ignite it. Always try to carry a little tinder with you. Larry usually grabs some birch bark. I have been using wax and sawdust fire starters that my wife buys at the grocery store to light our wood stove at home. I break them into small chunks that don't weigh much, but light easily and burn hot. I also keep a few paper towels handy. Keep all of the tinder in a plastic bag, or even two, so that it stays dry. Moisture has a way of working into everything on a wet day.

During a storm you can still find relatively dry wood under the branches of spruce or hemlock trees. The upper branches help to keep the snow or rain off the lower ones and usually they will be dry enough to burn. If you split the larger branches with your knife the inside wood will be dry and will light easier. Once you have a good

When choosing a butane lighter to carry for survival, pick one with a high flame. Bryce M. Towsley photo.

fire burning it will dry out the wood you add, so even wood that has been rained or snowed on will finally burn.

Try to find some shelter from the snow, rain, or wind. Moisture and wind will both rob you of body heat. If you need shelter quickly the best bet is to do like Larry did and burrow into the lower branches of a spruce tree. However, if you have a fire, be careful not to burn the tree. If you can find a crevice between a couple of rocks or ledges this makes a good place to escape the wind and the rocks will reflect the heat of the fire. If you carry one of the small, inexpensive space blankets it can be hung from branches and trees to act as a reflector as well. If you are between it and the fire both sides will stay warmer.

Don't try to make your way out in the dark—that's asking for trouble. You will increase the risk of poking a stick in your eye or falling down and getting hurt. You will also run the risk of becoming hopelessly lost. Stay put and wait for morning. If you hear shots, answer them, but stay put. Let your party come to you or at least know where you are so it can find you in the morning. It is not a bad idea to have a signal worked out with your partners to indicate if you need help or that you are all right. For years my family has used two fast shots followed by a single shot exactly 1 minute later to indicate that we need help. This is a shot pattern that is rarely heard during the daylight hours and is consequently easy to identify.

Shane looks on while Larry opens the chest cavity to allow access for cleaning and applying a salt-water solution. Benoit photo.

Don't worry too much about food or water. You may be hungry in the morning, but you won't starve to death. If you are cold, do not eat snow because that robs body heat.

Just remember it really isn't any different than being out in the woods during the daylight hours. You have no fears then, so don't have them at night. If you can survive during the day you can survive at night just as easily. Your biggest enemies are fear and your own mind. Think of it as an adventure. Stay calm, and morning will be along in a few hours. Then when you can see, you can find your way out.

Care of Meat

Never one to waste anything, Larry oversees the care of the bucks after they are tagged. When they go to Maine for a month at a time you would expect that there would be some problems in keeping the meat from spoiling, but that usually isn't the case at all.

Larry says, "When we field dress our deer we make a small cut and take out everything from the diaphragm back. The small hole keeps dirt, leaves, mud, and other junk from getting inside while we are dragging the buck out. Sometimes we have to drag them a long way and through some rough

Some 1988 bucks. Benoit photo.

country, so this is important. Once we get them back to camp and hung up we can then open them up a little more and clean out the chest and the pelvis area.

"It is important to cool the deer as soon as possible, but it is usually cold enough where we hunt that cooling the meat is not a problem. The bigger problem is keeping it from freezing before we can finish field dressing and preparing it to hang. On the other hand, if it is unseasonably warm we will try to get this done as fast as possible. If it is warm and we have to leave the deer in the woods we will open the chest cavity up and keep it propped open with a stick to aid in cooling the meat faster. The

A big buck ready for processing in Larry's living room. Benoit photo.

hide of a buck is a good insulator, it's what keeps them alive during those brutal winters so it has to be. To cool the deer, expose the open chest cavity to let the heat rise out. Otherwise the hide will trap it and spoil the meat.

"Back at camp we boil water and dissolve enough salt in it to float an egg. Using a brush, we will coat all the exposed meat including bullet holes with this solution. This helps to coat the meat, keeping insects and bacteria off it, particularly if it warms up. Then we hang the buck by its hind legs in a shady place. Because it is so cold in northern Maine or Vermont during the deer season the deer usually freezes. With the deer in the shade and well cooled or frozen, even if it warms up for a day or two they are fine. We just keep an eye on them.

"We let them hang for the rest of the season and take all our deer home intact at the end of the season. We then hang them on the porch of my house back in Vermont until we can process the meat. It is not unusual for a buck to hang a month before it is processed, but because it is so cold the meat is fine. I think it makes the meat better by aging it a little and tenderizing it.

"These old bucks lead a pretty easy life and the meat is surprisingly tender and good. There are exceptions of course, but we shoot only older trophy bucks and our meat is almost always excellent, tender, and tasty."

Cutting Them Up

You can pay somebody else to process your deer, but why would you want to? Not only will you wind up with better meat doing it yourself, but it's part of the hunt. Without the closure of processing the buck, the hunt again will seem diminished and incomplete.

Furthermore, a commercial processor often uses a power saw to cut the meat and this smears fat and bone marrow on the meat. Both are unpalatable and will ruin the taste of your steaks.

You don't need any fancy tools or a special work place. The Benoits process their bucks right in Lar-

ry's living room, from skinning to packaging. I skin mine in my back yard and process the meat at my kitchen table. All you will need are things you probably already have: a few knives, a cutting board, a saw, freezer wrap paper, tape, and a felt pen.

For skinning the deer, your hunting knife will work well. Additionally, when processing the meat, a fillet knife used for fish is helpful for boning, and a good butcher knife with a 7 or 8-inch blade to cut steaks will come in handy. Make sure that they are all shaving sharp.

The best cutting boards are made of plastic. You can buy these at any department store in the kitchen section. They are tough, won't dull your knife, and they will come clean easily. Wood is hard to clean and holds bacteria.

We will assume that you have split the buck up the belly and chest when you field dressed it. If you are planning to mount him make sure that you do not cut up the chest past the front legs, instead stay well behind them. Hang the buck by his back legs, cutting the skin between the tendon and the bone on the hock and inserting a gambrel or at least a stout stick. Make ringing cuts around all four legs above the knee joint. Then make a cut from these in a direct line to the open chest or belly. On the front legs, follow the cowlick that occurs where the white and brown hair meet. This is particularly important if you are going to mount the head.

Now, starting at those cuts on the buck's hindquarters, use your knife to cut the hide from the meat, pulling and working it off the deer. You will need to cut through the cartilage of the tail with a saw or hatchet to free it. Peel the hide off and down, cutting when necessary. Be careful not to leave any meat on the hide. You will find that you can angle the knife against the hide and, pulling on the hide to keep it taut, work the knife with short even strokes in a cutting motion so it separates the meat and hide cleanly. Be careful during all of this not to get any hair on the meat. If you find any, pick it off, because the hair will taint the meat and ruin the taste. Work carefully past the neck, taking caution not to make any cuts through the hide that the taxidermist will need to repair. At the base of the deer's head, cut through the neck to free the head and hide.

You don't need a special saw; a crosscut hand carpenter's saw works very well for cutting bone. It is best to take the hide and head to your taxidermist like this and let him finish caping the deer. If you cannot get it there very soon, put it in a double layer of garbage bags and freeze it. Do not put any salt on the hide. This can prevent it from freezing properly.

Now use the saw to cut the front legs off the deer above the remaining hide. Have one person hold the carcass while the other pulls the front leg away from it. Cut along the ribcage behind the front leg, in the "armpit" area with your knife, while pulling on the leg. This will allow you to cut the entire front shoulder free from the deer. Hold on, because it will be heavy when it comes free and be sure you have a clean, dry place to put it down. Now do the same with the other front shoulder.

Using your knife, cut along the backbone on each side to free the backstraps. These are the muscles that run on either side of the spine from the hind quarters to just behind the front shoulders. Using the edge of the muscle as a guide, work them free with your knife. When you are done you will have two pieces of meat that are oval in shape and about 15 inches long. Now use the saw to cut through the spine in front of the hind quarters to separate the hindquarters from the rest of the carcass. Again, it will be heavy when it is free.

Cut between the hind quarters until you separate the two and then cut the legs free just before the hide that is left below the knee joint. This will leave you with four quarters, two backstraps, and the ribcage. Free the neck from the ribcage as well as the tenderloins from inside the backbone in the gut cavity.

If you look at the muscle structure of the hindquarters you will see that the muscles can easily be separated from one another. Using your hunting knife and the fillet knife, do this and remove them from the bones, discarding the bone. Do the same with the front shoulders. Following the raised ridge off of the flat shoulder bone, you can work the fillet knife between the bone and the meat to separate the two. Remove all of the fat and connective membrane from all of the meat.

From here you have some choices on how you want the meat processed. The back straps are best if they are simply cut into 3/4-inch thick pieces to be used for chops or steaks. The same goes for the muscles from the hindquarters. Venison fat is not very palatable, so make sure you trim off all of the fat and connective tissue. A little extra time taken here will make much better tasting meat.

You might also consider using any of these pieces as a roast. Simply trim all of the fat and connective tissue, but leave the meat intact in the size roast you want.

The shoulders can be trimmed up and tied into roasts with string or cut into stew meat. The neck bone and windpipe can be removed and the neck used for roast.

Carefully trim all of the scraps and any meat you salvage from the ribcage into small pieces about a 1/2 inch square. Make sure all of the fat and gristle is removed. Use this meat for stew meat or to have ground into hamburger or sausage.

Double wrap the meat with freezer paper, tape it shut, and label it. Make several small packages rather than a few large ones. It is easier to thaw more than one package to adjust for your needs than to thaw one big package that is more than you need.

The meat will keep up to a year in a good freezer.

Cooking

Entire books have been written on cooking venison, and this is certainly no cook book, but here are a couple of our favorite recipes.

Remember that good venison is very lean and will overcook and dry out easily. Treat it like good beef and cook it with a red or pink center.

Shane likes to put the steaks in a frying pan with butter, salt, pepper, a little garlic, and perhaps onion. Fry on medium-high heat until the center is right and eat it hot. It's hard to find a better way to eat venison.

One of my favorite recipes was given to me by my friend Carl Beede:

For 2 pounds of venison combine:

1/3 cup of soy sauce
1/3 cup of brown sugar
1 tablespoon of minced onion
1/2 teaspoon of ginger
2 garlic cloves (crushed)
1/2 cup of cooking oil
2 bay leaves
1/2 cup of pineapple juice
Soak at least 48 hours and cook on the grill.

It is outstanding!

My mother used to prepare a roast by soaking it overnight in buttermilk. Then she would cover it with spicy sausage or bacon tied on with string and roast it in the oven until a meat thermometer showed the center was 140 degrees. I like it even better yet slow cooked in a crock pot.

Chapter 14

The End?

"It's up to us and nobody else. Is deer hunting important enough to you to work to save it?"

-Bryce M. Towsley

It is traditional to end a deer hunting book with a look to the future, but to be honest I am not all that optimistic, and when I look at what's ahead I don't like what I see. Hunting is on the ropes here, late in the second millennium, and it would take a catastrophic change to save it. American society has changed and, in most areas, not for the better.

There is a huge rising tide of animal rights proponents who are making inroads, both socially and legally. They are pushing their agendas against all hunting, trapping, and even eating meat with some surprising and disheartening success. Our rights to private ownership of firearms are being eroded on a parallel course that would have all gun owners now demonized in our society. This thinking is permeating entertainment, education, media, and just about all other segments of our society, which ensures that, as it becomes mainstream thinking, future generations will accept it without question.

Our children are being raised in different family structures and in a different culture than were past generations, most without the male role models who were pivotal in passing on the hunting traditions. As a result fewer and fewer of our youth are becoming deer hunters. As we age and our ranks thin through attrition, with nobody coming behind to fill the gaps, the sport of hunting will slowly just fade away.

Coupled with these threats are the loss of land, both as habitat and for hunting. Some is due to population growth, but even more is being lost to these same social changes. More and more land, both private and public, is being posted and removed from hunting, but the bigger threat may be the trend legislatively to confiscate private property rights from the land owners. Using environmental issues as a vehicle, certain factions are taking more and more of the rights of the landowners from them. As this continues and it becomes difficult economically to own property, a lot of it will revert to the government, and with current trends continuing, it is not likely that much of that land will be available for future generations to hunt.

It is a battle that was lost before it was started; we had everything to lose and they had everything to gain. It's like two children, one with a bag of candy and the other with nothing. Every time one takes some from the other, or is given some, the kid with the candy loses. Even if he grabs a little of it back he gains nothing. At best, he can get back what was his to start with.

We hunters are partly to blame, for many of us were so busy fighting among ourselves, or just focused on

Is this a sign of the future? Will there be anything left for the next generation? Bryce M. Towsley photo.

our own little world, that we didn't notice that there were forces out there trying to take all hunting away. We sat back and complacently let ourselves be led to the slaughter.

While it is doubtful that this can ever be reversed, we can stem the flow considerably. We can leave something for our children and grandchildren who want to be deer hunters. All it takes is for each of us to become involved. Let the politicians know how you feel, vote, stand up for our rights, and never, never apologize for being a deer hunter.

Finally, take some kids hunting and teach them about hunting. If you don't have any of your own, borrow a couple—it's a lot more fun when you get to give them back at the tired and cranky stage anyway. Even the little things count. My own son Nathan is 8 years old as I write this. He is a good little photography assistant and he worked with me on some of the photos you see in this book. On one trip to the Benoit's home, Larry gave him a key chain made from buckskin and a deer's antler. I don't think a pot of gold would be treasured so much, not so much for what it is, but more about who made it for him. That small gesture helped to steer him a little straighter down the path to becoming a deer hunter.

If we are going to see hunting survive at all we must involve the next generation. With the social changes of the last three decades there is no one else for many new hunters to learn from. It comes down to us. I started this book talking about the question, "If not now—when? If not us—who?" It was never so important as it is when applied to the next generation of deer hunters and who will teach them.

Are we so selfish that we would deprive them of the excitement of opening day and the anticipation that takes us there? Will we keep to ourselves the smell of a hardwood ridge on a damp November morning, the sight of the sun gleaming though the frost covering the tall grass at the edge of a beaver slough at daybreak, or of a buck silhouetted against the red morning sky? Will we hoard the beauty of the north country on a morning after a snowfall,

with its deep blue skies and air so cold that ice crystals hang in it like fairy dust to catch the light? Will we keep for ourselves the excitement of seeing a buck stepping down the trail, coming our way? Will we never share the thrill of sneaking up on a bedded 200-pound buck for the first time ever? Are we so stingy that we will keep only with ourselves that once in a lifetime excitement of a first deer?

If we truly love deer hunting the answer is obvious. The biggest thrill that many of us will ever experience is seeing the wonder and excitement reflected in the eyes of a hunter we are showing all of this to for the first time.

It's up to us and nobody else. Is deer hunting important enough to you to work to save it?

Shane Benoit. Bryce M. Towsley photo.

To close this book out we will leave the reader with this. For most hunters, there are two important days in the year and both carry a lot of meaning for a deer hunter: opening day when the excitement and anticipation have finally built to a crescendo, and the last day when it all comes crashing to an end.

Here are a few thoughts on those days. The first focuses on the necessity of having traditions in deer hunting, of sharing the sport with family and friends, and on the importance of passing these traditions on to the next generation. Part two looks at when it is over and how one deer hunter copes. At the same time it explores the ever-present optimism for next year, the never-ending hope and anticipation that all true deer hunters carry deep inside themselves.

Before

As the cold rain pounded the window the man stared without looking at the book in his lap.

He was thinking of that day so long ago when he took his first deer. He was 11 years old and it was his first year of hunting, but he wasn't thinking about the deer or his success. Instead he recalled the hug that his father gave him after he shot the deer. It was uncharacteristic of the man and its implications were not lost on his young mind. Even now, more than 30 years later he remembered that short hug as one of the best things his dad ever did.

As he wandered through the years that followed it seemed that he focused not on the deer he had taken, and there had been many, but on what really made deer hunting special in his life.

Lane's son Zeb is the latest generation of Benoit to show an interest in deer hunting. Will deer hunting be the same as we know it when he is old enough to hunt? Benoit photo.

He remembered how it felt to be invited to the family deer camp for the first time and how in awe of it all he was. He remembered the smell of the camp, a unique scent that even today he could identify blindfolded. He thought of how he felt, perched on the stairs to the sleeping loft and looking down at this group of men who he knew so well, yet who now seemed so strange. The man recalled listening so carefully to the stories his grandfather and the others were telling and to the rough jokes that he understood only to the extent that he knew by hearing them he was becoming accepted as one of the men. He again felt the strange longing to belong to this group, to fit in while at the same time knowing that his invited presence was a sign that he was on the road to that acceptance.

He thought of the excitement of the evening before the opening day and how the camp seemed to have a life of its own, one fed by the power of these men, a power too strong to be contained. It was, he knew now, the power of anticipation.

The man thought of the huge "grownup" breakfast the following morning and he tasted the bitterness of the coffee. His ears again heard the squeak of the snow as he and his dad left the camp in the dark and he felt the stark contrast of the clean fresh northern air to the humid and smoky interior of the camp. In his mind he was now out there on the edge of the hardwoods with his back against a big maple tree, and he was shivering, but not entirely from the cold. He felt the cold steel and the dark stained wood of that old Winchester he had held in his hands so long ago. He could sense the scent of his father hidden beside him in the darkness, mingling with the smell of his own freshly dry-cleaned wool coat.

The man remembered how as a boy he had tried so hard to please, to fit in, to be one of the guys, but how he was sure he had failed. He thought of the anxiety of this quest and how it seemed that he would never get it right. He couldn't know that only time could make it right, because to an 11 year old time is a strange concept.

How vividly he recalled the boredom that replaced the excitement as the day played out, and how it didn't seem to matter. He thought of the ex-citement and newness of all of the experiences; even getting the truck stuck in the mud was an adventure. He remembered the bear hanging from the meat pole as they pulled into camp that evening, and how it scared him as the headlights flashed across it.

The man thought of where that day had led him in his life. To the many hunts in distant places, how deer hunting had become such a large part of his life, his consuming passion. He thought of the places he had seen and the friends he had made and he was glad that life had taken the direction that it had. The man was thankful that he lived in a world with whitetail deer and that he was a part of those who hunted and loved them. The man pondered the question of how things might have played out if he had not been in that camp so long ago, if he had not been part of the tradition of deer season. He didn't like what he saw.

If deer hunting is to survive, we must make a greater effort to pass the traditions on to the younger generations. The author's son, Nathan Towsley, and his father-in-law, John Kascenska. Bryce M. Towsley photo.

The rain had changed to snow and the man turned his attention to it. He knew that the storm was to end by daybreak and that conditions would be good for hunting in the morning. He thought that he should join the rest of them in sleep because dawn was not far away, but he decided to sit and think a little longer.

There was much to consider, for tomorrow was opening day, and with his young son asleep in the loft, dreaming of his first day of deer hunting, he wanted to get it right.

After

Friends and relatives who have left for more temperate locations tell me that what they miss most about the Northeast is the four seasons.

I have a little trouble with that concept because I perceive each year as existing only within two seasons: deer season and whatever else there must be.

There was never a choice in what I have become and I can easily make a case for pre-destiny. I didn't choose deer hunting, it chose me. I can't even imagine my life if I were not a deer hunter. The very thought is as foreign to my consciousness as might be life as a woman. It is something that I believe I can understand intellectually, but that I will always fail to fully comprehend simply because it is so completely impossible.

I approach the fall season with an intensity that envelopes me completely. I don't and can't recognize the extent of this transition, simply because it is so complete. The flurry of activity from the first of October through mid-December is so intense, so passionate, that at times it threatens to consume me. While it may be apparent to those close to me, to me it never is obvious until later.

Each season is approached with an anticipation that builds and eases me into what is coming, but when it ends, it ends abruptly.

Regardless of where or when it happens, in each season there must always be a final day of hunting. When that day passes that's it, the end, finished. There is no transition, nothing to ease into the change, it just stops.

That's usually when it hits me how immersed in the hunting I have become. As I face the prospect of the end of another year of deer hunting, I realize just how much I have denied and dreaded this day. When it suddenly stops it creates a void, an emptiness within me that I can't understand, and I don't much like.

It doesn't matter how much hunting I have done in the season or how successful or unsuccessful I might have been, the results are still the same. My soul seems to exist as a vacuum and the emptiness leaves me restless and unable to focus.

For a while I wander through the days unable to concentrate or to channel my fragmented thoughts. I am irritable, short tempered, grumpy, and generally not at all pleasant to be around. I snap at my wife and ignore my kids.

Nothing really helps. I try reading books and magazines about deer hunting or watching videos, but find I can't concentrate. I spend time hunting coyotes or rabbits, but it's not the same.

I know that in time it will ease enough so I can function, but that it will not leave me completely. I have learned, if not to control it, to at least accept and live with it.

Much of this stems from the knowledge that each last day marks the passage of another year. It's a reminder that another hunting season is depleted from my life's allotment, and that the remaining stock is alarmingly low.

I know that I have consumed another opening day, that I have used the anticipation that precedes that day and I have lost the feelings and the excitement that exist only in the magic first moments of each season. It's all gone, used up, and it can't ever be replaced. I know that I have used more of the sights, the smells, and the feelings that are so subtle as to defy definition, and yet never fail to invoke strong emotions when they are encountered. I have again used some of my allocation of time in the woods that I so dearly love. The year's rations of friendship and camaraderie, along with the annual supply of campfires and nights with people I choose to spend time with, are depleted.

They cannot be stored or hoarded, yet so too are we unable to recover them. They are gone with the passage of time and like time they are gone forever. With each last day I am hitting my mortality head on.

I can't understand how time can be so different. It was such a short time ago, only a flash, an instant, that I watched dawn open the season for me and yet the next deer season is so far distant as to be almost inconceivable.

I know and understand that there are thousands of you out there who like me are suffering the same pains, but I also know, as do you, that as hunters we are solitary by nature and must endure this alone.

We take solace that, as impossible as it looks now, time will pass and another season will come. Hunting was meant to be used, to be consumed, to be experienced. This is the only way that deer hunting can exist, and by using and experiencing it we deer hunters justify and ensure our own existence, for without it we too will fail to exist.